What Do We
Tell The Children?

Books to use with children affected by illness and bereavement

Kerstin B Phillips

Published by
Paediatric AIDS Resource Centre (PARC), Edinburgh
Department of Child Life and Health
20 Sylvan Place
Edinburgh EH9 1UW
Tel: 0131 536 0806
Fax: 0131 536 0841

ISBN 1 900339 01 3

Foreword

When a child is affected by illness and bereavement they need all the help that adults can provide. But many people find it very difficult to know what to say, or what to do. Books can be of great assistance, whether they are books to read with a child or books to assist the adult helper.

This bibliography, 'What Do We Tell The Children?', will be of great help to many people in selecting suitable books. Its full description of the books will not only ensure that people are aware of what is available, but will enable the reader to make an appropriate selection for their individual and particular circumstances. 'What Do We Tell The Children?' is a much needed and long awaited resource.

Annabel Kanabus
Director
AVERT (AIDS Education & Research Trust)

Acknowledgements

I am grateful to the Paediatric AIDS Resource Centre (PARC) Edinburgh for enabling me to read such a variety of good books when I was commissioned to do this work. Without the help of librarians in Edinburgh, the task would have been impossible, especially Maggie Corr of Edinburgh City Libraries and several of the librarians in the School Library Service of Lothian Regional Council.

Contents

Introduction

"What shall we tell the children?" is a common plea for advice when parents, carers or teachers are told about a terminal condition in an adult or child, or when a family member has died. There is no straightforward answer to this question. There is nothing that anyone of us can say to a child that will remove the grief but, as adults we can help children to work through their grief by encouraging them to talk about feelings, by listening, and by giving the child time and space for the personal work that has to be done.

For many of us it is difficult to find the words to use when talking with someone facing loss and pain. It can be very difficult to identify feelings and name them, especially as so many of the feelings experienced when grieving are perceived to be negative. Children may find this even more difficult than adults.

Reading a book or having a book read aloud can be a helpful way of starting to talk about feelings. Through a fictional character we can compare, recognise, reject or agree with the feelings expressed through the words or actions in the book. It is reassuring to read about someone else being as confused or angry, especially when one thinks there are subtle rules for how one should feel or behave. Sharing a book with a trusted adult can encourage a child to start talking. The book does not necessarily have to deal with an identical situation: indeed, it may feel safer if it is about a different situation.

The books included in this bibliography have been selected because they deal with grief and loss. The aim has been to identify books that can be used with children of different age groups and includes fiction and information books. Many children are suffering bereavement through a parent or close relative dying of AIDS and books on HIV and AIDS are also included.

There are a number of books in this bibliography to help the adult understand something of how children grieve. Some are written for parents and carers, others are written for professionally trained workers. I have included an anthology of poems and prose and there are some books written for and by bereaved parents.

Children may be attending clinics, having short stays in hospital or be visiting a relative in hospital. There are a number of picture books to help prepare a child for what to expect, giving information about what they might see, what the different professionals are called and about some of the medical procedures people undergo while in hospital.

There have been requests from teachers supporting a bereaved pupil, or those who want to plan some input into their Personal and Social Education sessions on loss and bereavement as suitable resources. Some schools also want to prepare a plan of how to respond to a crisis situation involving the death of one or more pupils, so I have included some books that may be of help in these situations.

Advice to the adult helper

Many adults faced with a grieving child don't know what to say: they fear that they might say or do the wrong thing. Most adults recognise that grieving children need to mourn but do not know how to help and support a child. There is no single or right path through grief work – each person going through loss and bereavement makes their own personal journey. A child's experience will depend on developmental stage, previous experience and level of understanding. Children often do not express grief in the same way as adults do, or as adults think they should. Their feelings fluctuate and their attention span can be very short, especially when something traumatic has happened. The way the family thinks and behaves around illness and death is important, even if family members have not openly shared their views. Attitudes in families are themselves influenced by previous generations, and by social, religious or cultural influences.

Parents, carers, social workers and teachers have asked for books that can be used with a particular child – not necessarily for a book to be read alone but for one to be read together with the child. When distressed, a child can find it difficult to talk about feelings, and it may be impossible even to identify what they are. Some children find it easier to talk about a fictional character in a book, and may compare the experiences or feelings of the character with what they themselves are feeling. Sharing a book together can make it possible for the adult helper to encourage the child to start talking about feelings and worries. A child may feel reassured to read about a character in a book expressing confusion, fear and anger or withdrawing from the rest of the family. However, if a book is to be useful for therapeutic purposes, the story should move on to offer some hope that feelings can change, and should perhaps also show the beginning of some understanding of the situation.

However, the story in the book is fiction and the child to be helped will have to find his or her own ways through pain and confusion. The child must feel encouraged to express feelings that may or may not agree with those in the story.

A teenager often finds it even more difficult than younger children to talk with an adult helper. By reading a novel suggested by the adult, the teenager may be able to agree or disagree with the feelings expressed, may recognise some of the situations and possibly find comfort from the experiences of the fictional characters. It may feel safer to express anger or grief on behalf of people in the book rather than on behalf of his or her own experience. The teenager may then take an opportunity offered by the adult to discuss the book and possibly share some of the feelings. However, the teenager may want to choose when and where and with whom this work can start, and the intensity of the contact.

HIV/AIDS

In Lothian we have become aware of a growing need for books to help children who are bewildered and suffering loss of their family environment when someone close to them has developed AIDS or has died. There are also a considerable number of children and young people who are affected by having a close family member infected with HIV, an infection surrounded by stigma.

As this project is sponsored by the Paediatric AIDS Resource Centre (PARC) in Edinburgh, there is a section of books dealing with HIV, both fiction as well as non fiction books, written for children and young adults.

The majority of the books listed do not deal with HIV/AIDS specifically but the feelings and experiences are often similar for children and adults touched by a variety of chronic or terminal conditions. The emotions that children and adults experience are similar whether the cause is cancer or AIDS, and so the list can be a useful resource whatever the cause of the bereavement.

Parents living with HIV have asked for books to help them open up this topic with their own children, and for books that will help them to explain how the virus works.

Many teenagers choose to do a project on HIV/AIDS at school: this may be a means of coming to terms with their own fears about HIV, or may simply result from their increased awareness about HIV infection and its social implications. Teachers, who suspect or know that someone in the class is affected by HIV in their family, may want unobtrusively to include some factual book on HIV on the shelves of the class library. There are books included to help with this.

How to use this book list

The reviews are arranged alphabetically according to the title. Identify a number of possible books from the reviews, borrow them and read them yourself first. Some of the books are out of print but your local library may have many of them or will be able to get them through an inter-library loan. School libraries also have a number of books that may no longer be available in bookshops.

How to select a book appropriate for the child in question

The adult selecting books for a distressed child must read the book beforehand and plan how the book should best be used. Many children and adults like to have a book read to them while they are relaxing in a comfortable chair. A young child may want to sit on your lap. Plan to leave time to talk about what you have read together, share your own feelings as appropriate, but do not assume that you know what the child feels. Do not project your feelings onto the child. Wait and listen. The child may express feelings in words, in behaviour or through drawings, in ways that are new to the adult. Feelings are neither right nor wrong – they just are what they are, and they need to be acknowledged. It is how we act on them that can be helpful or harmful.

The attention span of a confused or grieving child will be much shorter than one might expect. If you find that the child does not like the book, don't persevere, choose a different book or leave it for another time. Many parents have probably had the experience of giving their child a book they used to love when they were the same age, only to find that their own child rejects the book as being too childish or boring. If the child does not engage with the book, this should be accepted.

There are only a few books in this list written for children and young adults with special educational needs. They may find some of the Picture Books helpful.

When trying to categorise the books, I have labelled some books as touching on bereavement. The label is there to help you avoid books for which the child may not yet be ready. When children are starting to deal with the feelings around a chronic or terminal condition, they may not want to face the fact that death may be the outcome. If that is so, avoid those books that deal with bereavement.

Age grouping

Age references are only guidelines. A distressed child may regress and find a book aimed at a younger child more useful, so both teenagers and adults may find some of the Picture Books very helpful. A child who normally does not enjoy reading may also prefer a book with illustrations where feelings and events are depicted visually.

The books selected

This is not a comprehensive list. I am aware that there is a lack of books in this collection that reflect how the major religions support their children through bereavement. It has also been difficult to find books where the story deals with children from different ethnic groups.

There are many books that deal with the death of a grandparent and only a few of those have been selected. The aim has been to concentrate on books for children who grieve for a parent or sibling and where death happens before the end of the normally expected lifespan. There are also picture books introducing death to young children through the death of a pet. In some of them the dead pet is replaced by a new one at the end of the story. This is not helpful for a child who has lost a parent.

Inevitably the list is only a selection of books available at the time of writing and which have been recommended by friends, librarians or authors. There are books missing because they could not be located and read within the time available. There are bound to be many appropriate books that have not been included in this first edition. If you have found a particular book useful which is not included, PARC would be grateful for the information.

Some of the books included exist in several editions, and books out of print at the moment may be re-issued. In the case of some picture books, the text is occasionally accompanied by new illustrations. The price is included as a guide to the cost but it may also vary from that which has been given here.

Medical information and publishing date

When selecting a book that deals with a medical condition such as HIV, it is quite important to check the date of publication. A book published in a particular year will reflect knowledge and attitudes prevalent at the time of writing, ie a year or two earlier. Medical knowledge, treatment and prognosis are changing rapidly in regards to several chronic or terminal conditions. If a particular book contains even some information that is now regarded as out of date, leave that book aside.

Support for the adult helper

If you are affected yourself, find some support and talk through what you want for your child and how you plan to approach it. The telephone directory is often a good source of information of agencies available locally.

Agencies:
Cruse
Compassionate Friends
Samaritans
GP surgery
Health visitor
Libraries
Voluntary agencies that specialise in the syndrome or condition in question

The views expressed are those of the reviewer and are not necessarily those of PARC.

Kerstin B Phillips
Edinburgh, 1995

Book titles according to contents and reader age

The age groupings are tentative.
Books written for younger children may also be appropriate.

Books indicated with * touch on HIV, and the symbol # indicates
that the book also deals with death.

Feelings

Primary age children, picture books

Books dealing with visits to the clinic or hospital

Pre-school children, picture books

Primary age children, picture books

Serious illness

Many of the books under the HIV and loss and bereavement headings are also very appropriate.

Interactive work book for a child to use with an adult:

Primary age children

Early teens

Adults

Fiction books dealing with HIV and AIDS

Primary age children, picture books

Pre-teens

Early teens

Late teens

Information books on HIV and AIDS

Interactive work book for a child to use with an adult:

Primary age children

Early teens

Early and late teens

Late teens

Adults

Information books for children dealing with bereavement and loss

Interactive work books for a child to use with an adult:

Primary age children

Early teens

Early and late teens

Late teens

Books for adults helping children deal with bereavement and loss

Fiction for children dealing with bereavement and loss

Pre-school children, picture books

Primary age children, picture books

Upper primary school age

Early teens

Late teens

Books for teachers planning to help children at school cope with bereavement and loss

Book reviews in alphabetical order according to title

It may be possible to borrow out of print books from a library.

A Formal Feeling
Zibby O'Neal
Armada Books, 1985   0 00 672291 1   Out of print

Anne, who is at boarding school in America, returns home for Christmas. It is a year since her mother died and her father has remarried. Anne feels angry and bewildered, and cannot respond to the approaches made by her older brother. She feels that all have forgotten her accomplished, beautiful and perfect mother yet there seems to be gaps in her memory. During the Christmas holiday memories slowly return and by the end of it she is able to see the people around her realistically and her alienation is broken.

A sensitive book for young teenagers.

A Handbook on Death and Bereavement: Helping children understand
Beverley Mathias, Desmond Spiers
The National Library for the Handicapped Child, 1992
Reach Resource Centre, Wellington House, Wellington Road,
Wokingham, Berks RG11 2AG   0 948664 10 X   £2.95

This is a list of 113 books which deal with death and bereavement for children. The books are reviewed and classified according to interest levels: Pre-school, Infant, Lower Primary, Upper Primary, Secondary and Adult reference. There is an index where the reader can find books covering a specific topic such as accidental death, explaining death, death of a particular relative, terminal illness, etc. There is also a list of organisations and their addresses.

A very useful reference book for adults.

A Rock and a Hard Place

Anthony Godby Johnson

Little, Brown and Company, 1993   0 316 90690 5   £12.95

This is written by an American teenage boy dying of AIDS who was physically, mentally and sexually abused by his parents and others throughout his childhood. In different chapters he describes a series of people regarded by others as marginal who have revealed their specialness to him. He also describes his own life of absolute despair before being rescued by telephoning an advice line for teenagers. He is befriended by the person who answered the call for help who then adopts him. This man then marries another of the boy's befrienders. The author became infected by a person with AIDS who assaulted him with his parents permission.

For older teenagers.

A Sound of Chariots

Molly Hunter

Magna Print Books (large print)	1 85057 183	£8.95
Collins Lions, 1988	0 00 672092 7	Out of print

Bridie McShane grew up in a poor village close to the Firth of Forth in Scotland after World War I, the youngest of four sisters and the most sensitive of the children. Her beloved father is a war veteran, Bridie being his special child. When he dies Bridie changes through her own grief and from observing other people around her. It is a most moving and haunting book full of compassion. The story is a powerful description of life amongst a small settlement of war wounded. It vividly describes the raw feelings of Bridie and her mother when the father dies. Bridie becomes aware of time passing and the reality of her own eventual death.

Highly recommended for younger teenagers.

A Star for the Latecomer

Paul Zindel, Bonnie Zindel

Red Fox, 1991   0 09 987200 5   £2.99

When 16 year-old Brooke discovers her mother is dying from cancer, she is torn between trying to fulfil her mother's dream and become a 'star' and trying to understand how she can achieve her own dream of happiness within a relationship in the future. The book describes a loving and supportive but, also suffocating, relationship between Brooke and her mother. The mother is slowly getting more ill and she changes both emotionally and physically. Brooke finally gets strength to make her own decisions.

This book could be helpful for a younger teenage girl whose mother is terminally ill.

A Summer to Die

Lois Lowry

Collins Lions, 1990   0 00 673598 3   Out of print

Meg has a pretty and popular older sister, Molly, who is 15. The whole family moves to the country for a year so that the father will have peace to complete writing a book. Meg is plain and serious and develops her talent for photography but is quite jealous of Molly's social ease. Meg becomes ill with leukaemia and life changes for the whole family. Meg has made a good friend in an old man living nearby and has developed a friendship with a young couple who ask her to be present when their child is born. Meg dies in hospital after a slow and steady deterioration.

The book deals gently with the difficult feelings between two teenage sisters who share a room. It takes some time before Molly realises how ill Meg really is and the reason why her parents' behaviour has changed so much. This is a book that could be very helpful for a young teenager who has to face a similar situation.

A Taste of Blackberries

Doris Buchanan Smith

Penguin, 1987   0 14 032020 2   £3.25

Two boys of early primary school age live next door to each other and are in and out of each other's houses – they always play together. Jamie loves fooling about and playing jokes. When he gets stung by a bee one day, nobody pays much attention to his behaviour: but he dies and his best friend tries to bring him back by refusing to eat, and by staying apart from those around him. His loving parents and neighbours support him unobtrusively and he finally finds a way of making contact with Jamie's mother by picking blackberries for her.

A sensitive book dealing with grief for children of upper primary school age. This could be very useful to read with a child at home or at school especially when a class mate has died. The book has pen illustrations.

AIDS
Alison and David Kilpatrick

Chambers Teenage Information series, 1987 0 550 75224 2   £2.25

The book talks about 'risk groups', AIDS carriers and AIDS victims which are dated terms. It wrongly states that there is a high risk of vertical transmission from a mother to her baby and that AIDS in heterosexuals is not common outside Africa. The discussion about whether healthy carriers will die before their time or not is unhelpful. The discussion of homosexual behaviour may cause offence. This book reflects the fact that it was written in the early days of the epidemic and should not be used any more. It is aimed at teenage readers.

AIDS and Children: What's it got to do with them?
AVERT

11 Denne Parade, Horsham 1994, West Sussex RH12 1JD   £0.42

A small booklet of 24 pages giving simple information about HIV and AIDS, about how to reduce the risk of infection as well as some suggestions on how to talk to children. It is written for adults working with children and concerned with their welfare. It introduces some of the important issues round confidentiality by pointing out that individuals have a right to privacy and discusses what to do if someone tells you about the HIV status of a child and whether you should tell others. It considers the needs of children living with HIV and the fact that all children are affected by AIDS as they hear about it and can become confused and worried. There is advice on what to think through before talking with a child and where to find out more about HIV. Appendix A deals with basic facts about HIV and Appendix B gives the recommended good hygiene procedures.

The booklet is easy to read and the excellent text is well presented. Because of the low price, all who work with children could be given a copy of this useful booklet.

AIDS and Families:
Report of the AIDS Task Force, Groves Conference on
Marriage and the Family

Ed: Eleanor D Macklin

Harrington Park Press, 1989   0 918393 60 4   £12.50

This is a collection of articles written by a variety of specialists in America, in the late 1980s, for family professionals, to stimulate the planning of services. Family is defined in broad terms and can consist of family of procreation, couples and friendship networks and the caregivers. The factual information reflects the knowledge and issues at the time and references are to American public policies. Some of the contributions are still relevant – the guidelines for education and service delivery are as thought provoking now as then.

AIDS in the Family:
Information for parents and carers of children

Barnardo's/The Terrence Higgins Trust

The Terrence Higgins Trust, 1991
52–54 Grays Inn Road, London WC1X 8JU

A 23 page leaflet giving information about HIV and AIDS to families and households with children where there is an infected family member. There is a chapter on talking with children about HIV and about support for children. There are also relevant addresses. A useful booklet.

AIDS in the Family

Libby Spurrier

Hodder, 1993   0 340 58973 6   £9.99

The book starts off with a good glossary and then with factual information. This is followed by a dozen case stories told by close relatives who have nursed an adult family member with AIDS, usually in London. It deals with the feelings and experiences they have had as siblings, partners or parents from when the diagnosis was revealed to them and onwards. This book could be useful for adult carers in that they might recognise their own experiences and feelings.

AIDS

Graham Wilkinson

'Let's Discuss' series, Wayland, 1987   1 85210 295 0   Out of print

The series aims to stimulate questioning and discussion of important social issues. The text explains what is known about HIV infection and how young people can reduce their risk of infection. There are fictitious case stories and finally an examination of the social, medical and political problems society faces while attempting to cope with AIDS.

There are factual errors, ie 'only 15 per cent of those infected with HIV go on to develop AIDS'. Figures are those of 1987 and thus far out of date. It is suggested that prostitutes may be an important source of HIV.

The author is an AIDS counsellor. For younger teenagers.

AIDS

Pete Sanders, Clare Farquhar

'Let's Talk About' series,
Gloucester Press, 1994   0 7496 2068 4   £4.50

The text is printed on one side with a colour photograph opposite on each double spread. It starts with information about how to avoid HIV infection and continues with simple information about AIDS, drugs, making love (but without any details), photographs of condoms, advice groups, research into treatment and finally a chapter, 'What can I do?' The language is easy and there is not too much text. There is a glossary at the end as well as telephone numbers. It is written by a primary school teacher and an educational psychologist specialising in primary education. Suitable for a primary school library.

AIDS: The ultimate challenge

Elisabeth Kübler-Ross

Collier Paperbacks (1987), 1993   0 02 089143 1   £6.95

'Is it possible that our AIDS patients, children and adults alike, chose to contribute their short life-spans on planet Earth to help us open our eyes, to raise our consciousness, to open our hearts and minds, and to finally see the light?' The book was written in the early years of the pandemic and reflects attitudes and experiences in America at that time. The author, who is a

Christian doctor, now runs bereavement courses all over the world and has written several books about death and dying. She comforts the dying and the book contains stories of gay men living in isolation and despair until she or other volunteers intervene. She wants parents to become like parents used to be and take time to listen to their children long before they are dying – this may have enabled homosexuals to stay in monogamous relationships. Busy materialistic parents have not given unconditional love and not educated their children about drug misuse, have done a poor job with sex education and have shown little understanding for their youngsters. She also describes the selfless care some mothers show when their child is dying. She advises parents planning to adopt to request a blood test. Infected haemophiliacs should refrain from marrying. Female prostitutes are blamed. A large part of the book is taken up with a verbatim record of a meeting held locally when she was attempting to build a hospice for AIDS babies and the letters written to the local paper opposing this. She pleads for tolerance and acceptance of people with AIDS.

The book is an often moving historical record of her and her friends' experiences with young gay men dying of AIDS in America in the mid 1980s.

AIDS – Trading Fears for Facts: A guide for young people

Karen Hein

Consumer Reports Books, NY, 1991   0 89043 481 6   Out of print

An American book written for American teenagers about AIDS. It does not deal with bereavement.

AIDS: You can't catch it holding hands

Niki de Saint-Phalle

The Lapis Press, San Francisco US, 1987   0 932499 52 X   Out of print

A book written and illustrated by a famous artist for an adult, American audience too long ago. It contains a number of statements that are dubious or unacceptable now such as ' in intestinal secretions and even tears', 'faithful couples can't catch it', 'sex parties are OK', 'reduce your number of lovers as much as possible', 'no saunas, no bath houses', '+ve men should not have children'. The book is artistic to look at but inappropriate for children and factually incorrect in several places.

All in the End is Harvest:
An anthology for those who grieve
Ed: Agnes Whitaker

Darton Longman and Todd in association
with Cruse, 1994   0 232 51624 3   £8.95

A collection of poetry and prose about death and grief expressing emotions such as fear, despair, anger, bereavement and rage. There are also positive emotions – lives celebrated with triumph, joy and delight. One of the themes is hope: hope that even though the grief is bad, it has a meaning, hope that some good can come out of the love, hope that all is not chaos. The anthology consists of passages selected from books and letters, both in English and in translation from other languages. This is a book to be dipped into over a long period of time.

Am I Allowed to Cry? A study of bereavement amongst people who have learning difficulties
Maureen Oswin

Souvenir Press, 1991   0 285 65096 3   £7.99

The author has interviewed family members where there is a child with profound learning difficulties who has suffered bereavement, as well as residents and staff in a variety of residential homes. She reveals the distressing lack of understanding by professionals of the needs of those bereaved; she also suggests that feelings and grieving behaviour are similar in all human beings. There are guidelines for encouraging change and improvement in staff training on how to deal supportively with bereaved children and adults.

This book is a plea for better understanding of the needs of those with profound learning difficulties who suffer bereavement. It would be useful for those who work with or have to give advice on how to support very vulnerable individuals who may not easily make themselves understood.

Anatomy of Bereavement:
A handbook for the caring professions
Beverley Raphael
Routledge, 1992   0 415 09454 2   £16.99

A comprehensive book covering the field of bereavement, thoroughly underpinned by references to different studies and deeply rooted in the author's practical experiences of working with bereaved people.

The author starts by looking at human bonds within the nuclear family and beyond, and how they affect the experience of loss and the perception of death. She goes on to deal with separation and mourning. In a useful chapter on the bereaved child the experiencing of loss and grief by children of different ages is described. This is followed by grief and mourning as experienced by teenagers. Loss in adult life is covered in chapters on the death of a spouse, on the death of a child, and the grief of growing old. There is a chapter on disasters causing trauma for a large number of individuals at the same time, and others on how to care for the bereaved, offer comfort and facilitate recovery. The last couple of pages deals with living with loss.

The author is a professor of psychiatry. This is a comprehensive and scholarly book with case studies, dialogues and quotes. It is regarded by many professionals as an excellent and essential book for those working with bereaved persons. It is a book that can be referred to frequently.

Badger on the Barge
Janni Howker
Julia MacRae Books, 1984   0 86203 163 X   £7.95

A book of short stories where the first one deals obliquely with grief in a family. Helen's big brother is killed in a motorcycle accident and her father has withdrawn completely from her and his wife. Helen gets involved with an isolated old woman on a barge who keeps a badger. Through the reluctant friendship that develops between the woman and the teenage girl Helen's father is brought out of his isolation and grief.

The stories are well written and the few characters in each are well drawn and their feelings described sensitively – a book difficult to put down. Written for teenagers.

Badger's Parting Gifts

Susan Varley

Picture Lions (1984) new edition   0 00 662398 0   £3.99

Old Badger knew that he must die soon and feels ready for it. Dying is described as running with ease down a long tunnel. His friends are sad, feeling lost and unhappy. However, with time they remember all the nice things Badger had taught them and they each have a special memory of Badger: these were his parting gifts, to treasure for always and share with others.

This is a comforting and lovely picture book recommended by teachers in primary schools who have used it with their 4–10 year-old pupils.

Becca's Race

Bette Paul

Scholastic Children's Books, 1992   0 590 55052 7   £4.99

Digby who is going to do his GCSEs has an admired big sister who develops leukaemia. The book deals with how the family members react to the stress as Becca becomes more ill and undergoes chemotherapy and then a bone marrow transplant. It also deals with Digby's first tentative relationship with a girl at school where they are both outsiders.

This teenage book reads well and deals with serious illness and the family stress caused by it.

Beginnings and Endings with Lifetimes In-between

Bryan Mellonie, Robert Ingpen

Dragon's World Ltd, 1987   1 85028 038 X   Out of print

'There is a beginning and an ending for everything that is alive. In between is living. All around us, everywhere, beginnings and endings are going on all the time.'

This is a beautifully illustrated book with clear, realistic pictures and a well thought out short text on each double page. It details a variety of animal and plant lives and finishes off with humans, some of whom have a lifespan of more years, others with fewer years.

A highly recommended book for very young children and upwards, maybe even for adults. This could be used with a child with special educational needs.

Bereavement – Help for the family who have lost a CF child
Janet Goodall
City General Hospital, North Staffs Hospital Centre, 1988
Stoke-on-Trent, ST4 6QG
Cystic Fibrosis Research Trust
Alexandra House, 5 Blyth Road, Bromley, Kent

A small booklet of 13 pages written for parents who have lost a child. It is used when counselling bereaved parents and has been adapted to include some of their suggestions.

The booklet deals with feelings and people adjusting to the loss, parents who misunderstand each other when they may react differently, the needs of other children and the needs of relatives and friends feeling helpless and not knowing what to say. There are sources of help available.

A very useful booklet for parents. There is no reference to CF other than in the title.

Bridge to Terabithia
Katherine Paterson
Puffin Books (1986) new edition   0 14 031260 9   £3.50

Two young teenage outsiders in the American outback become friends and start playing splendid games in their secret country on an island in the creek. Both of them escape their difficulties, at home and in school, in their imaginary kingdom of Terabithia. Towards the end of the book Leslie drowns when she swings across the creek to the island and Jess is left stunned. In his grief he slowly learns to accept help from his family. Written for children of upper primary school age.

Caring for Bereaved Children

Mary Bending

Cruse Bereavement Care, 1993
126 Sheen Road, Richmond, Surrey,
England TW9 1UR   0 900321 06 7

A small book of 28 pages for adults who care for bereaved children either as a parent, relative or teacher. This is a very helpful book, short and easy to read when an adult wants sensible advice on how to help a child in an immediate situation. It also introduces how children of different ages, from birth to adolescence, understand death and how they may react. A highly recommended little book.

Caring for Children with HIV and AIDS

Ed: Rosie Claxton and Tony Harrison

Edward Arnold, 1991   0 340 55256 5   £13.99

A comprehensive book written by professionals from a variety of backgrounds for medical personnel, social workers and those involved in child care organisations. It covers epidemiology, the care and medical management of children with HIV, legal and ethical issues, pregnancy and childbirth, caring and nursing of children with HIV, social care of families affected by HIV, neuropsychological assessment and psychological support of families and children. A very moving part of the book consists of the personal thoughts of some families affected by HIV. There is a resource list of organisations.

This book is for specialists.

Children and the AIDS Virus

Rosemary Hausherr

Clarion Books, New York, 1989   0 395 51167 4   Out of print

The book starts off with the body and microbes which can cause illness such as the cold virus and its symptoms. It moves on to talk about a new virus, HIV. The book lists ways in which you, as a child, cannot get infected, but also makes clear that it is spread through needle sharing and having sex. In the sub-text, condoms are mentioned. Jonathan, who is 5 and enjoys flying paper aeroplanes, has AIDS because of an infected blood transfusion. He goes to school and plays with his friends. Celeste was born with the AIDS virus. Both these children are helped by doctors and nurses but there is no cure.

The book does not distinguish between HIV and AIDS.

At the back there is factual information about Jonathan and his family, and Celeste and her grandmother. The book is American so the resource list is not useful here. It is a warm and friendly book to read for a family with an infected child. It is illustrated with multicultural photographs on each double page spread.

This is a book to be read with a young child. Information for the parent, or older child is printed in smaller text below the text you would read to the child.

Ciara's Story

Grace FitzGerald
Irish Association of Social Workers
114 Perse St, D2, Eire   0 86387 032 5

Ciara is six years old and she goes for a check-up to hospital every month. The doctor tells her about HIV in her blood and she has tests. Once she even stayed in hospital and was given medicine through a drip. She became better and went home and all were happy to see her again.

This is a colourful and reassuring picture book for a child with HIV.

It can be used as a reading aloud book for young children or for slightly older children to read themselves.

Come Back, Grandma

Sue Limb
Bodley Head, 1993   0 370 31807 2   £8.99

Bessie loves and is loved by Mummy and Daddy but both are busy. Grandma was always there for doing special things with, she always had time for Bessie but one day she died. Bessie missed her and sometimes thought she could see her. Bessie tried to see heaven where Mummy said Grandma was. Daddy said Grandma was now part of nature. Krishna next door said Grandma might be reborn as an animal but Bessie couldn't see her anywhere. Bessie grew up, and still missed Grandma sometimes. Later she married and had a baby and as the baby grew up, she grew to look a bit like Grandma and this stopped Bessie feeling sad.

A big picture book for younger children of school age.

Come Sit By Me

Margaret Merrifield

Women's Press, Canada, 1990   0 88961 141 6   £3.50

An attractive picture book about Karen and her friends in nursery school. Nicholas is a new child who is sometimes off ill. He has got AIDS. Karen's mother explains that his fighter cells can't help him get better. She also tells Karen that she can play, eat with, sleep beside him, hug him and play like any other friend: she does and has no worries. There is a meeting for parents where they learn about AIDS and after that Nicholas is completely accepted by the children.

At the end of the book there is a double page spread with attractive pictures showing all the activities that do not spread HIV. Finally there are a couple of pages of facts for adults.

An excellent book suitable for young children of nursery age or primary school age who may be in contact with someone with HIV.

Dance on my Grave

Aidan Chambers

Red Fox, 1995   0 09 950291 7   £3.99

The novel is about the relationship between a 16 year-old boy Hal and an older teenage boy, Barry, which lasted for seven intensive weeks before the older boy dies in a motorbike accident. The story is written by Hal in order to come to terms with what has happened. It starts out with his search in early childhood for a close friend and the frequent let downs until the day he is rescued in a sailing accident by Barry. Their relationship soon develops into a physical one. Hal is a sensitive teenager, interested in ideas. In his search for the perfect friend he creates a fantasy image of Barry. At the end of the book, Hal has learnt a lot about himself and about those around him. Barry's death is a theme which runs right from the beginning of the book and throughout the narrative.

A sensitive, mature book for older teenagers.

Dead Birds Singing

Marc Talbert

Penguin, 1988   0 14 032184 5   Out of print

Matt, of early secondary school age, lives with his mother and older sister. He and his best friend, Jamie, are in a swimming team together. Coming back in the car from a competition he had just won, there is an accident and his mother dies at once, and his sister after some time. Matt is taken home by Jamie's parents who were close family friends. He is angry, confused, lonely and grieving as well as having to adjust to living in a new family. He is eventually offered a permanent home there and is supported both by his friend and the parents to deal with his bitter feelings.

This is a powerful story about the feelings when you are bereaved but also about the realistic difficulties when adjusting to living in with a new family. A well written book for 10–14 year olds.

Death and Dying

Pete Sanders

'Let's talk about' series
Franklin Gloucester Press, 1990   0 7496 0431 X   £7.99

The text with multicultural colour photographs covers chapters on 'What is death?', 'What is dying'?, 'What happens after?' Feelings of anger, guilt, worry, feeling sad for a long time and the embarrassment at expressing real feelings in public are written about and illustrated. Each chapter is a two page spread. The telephone number to Childline as well as a glossary are at the end of the book. The book is written by a primary school teacher for children between 5–12 and is well researched. Suitable for the school library.

Death and Loss – Compassionate approaches in the classroom

Oliver Leaman

Cassell, 1995   0 304 33089 2   £12.99

This book is written by a philosopher concerned with integrating teaching about death in schools. There are a number of transcriptions of interviews with children of different ages on their perceptions of death, included to illustrate the point that all children need to be helped to reflect on death since death comes to everyone. Education about death should enable pupils to assess their own risk taking. Only when a person's attitude to death is clearer can he or she take rational decisions about preferred activities and take increasing control of his or her life. Pupils need to be given opportunities to develop their own views on their future and what risks they wish to take with the assistance of their teachers. The book deals with the attitude of schools and teachers to death, talking to children about death and risk, disasters and ordinary tragedies and how to incorporate this into the curriculum.

This is a thoughtful and well reasoned book about the need to help children adjust to loss and grief, written for teachers involved in planning the pastoral care of pupils.

Death Customs
Jon Mayled
Religious Topics series, Wayland, 1986   0 85078 719 X   £5.50

Colour photographs on each page help to explain rituals and how death is understood in different religious traditions. Each religion has three or four pages of simple text. Those covered are Buddhism, Chinese tradition, Taoism, Christianity, Hinduism, Islam, Judaism and Sikhism. There is a glossary at the back.

This is a good resource book for a primary school library, to be used especially when someone in the class is going through bereavement.

Death
Karen Bryant-Mole
'What's Happening' series
Wayland (1992) new edition   0 7502 1379 5   £4.50

A book with text and multicultural photographs that deal with different children experiencing the death of a dog, a great grandmother, a mother, a dad and siblings. The text deals with feelings of fear, nightmares, and confusion. It talks about how to handle hurt and anger, mixed up feelings and being upset. There is a chapter on funerals and 'Who will take care of me'. It emphasises the importance of talking about feelings and about the dead person. It suggests that some children could draw when it is difficult to talk.

There are special occasions for remembering those who have died, and to share important memories.

An excellent book for older primary school age children.

Death: The final journey?
Linda Smith

Lion Educational, 1990   0 7459 1336 9   £2.95

This is one title in the series of Topic Books designed for Personal and Social Education and Religious Education in secondary schools. Each chapter uses a variety of presentations to give facts and personal stories followed by work assignments. The topics cover death, euthanasia, how people respond to death and life after death. The final section covers the Christian view of death, resurrection and Jesus.

A useful information book to use in a class studying issues round death and bereavement. For teenagers.

Dicey's Song
Cynthia Voight

Lions (1990) new edition   0 00 672566 X   £3.99

Dicey is a young teenage girl who brought her three younger siblings to their grandmother when their mother became mentally ill and hospitalised. The four children and their grandmother had never met each other before. The story deals with all of them having to adjust to living with each other in rural America. Dicey continues to feel responsible for her younger sister and brothers. Each of them have their personal problems and deep insecurities. Dicey, who has had to take on far too much responsibility, finds it difficult to get on with the others at school and she continues to worry about the younger ones. The grandmother, who has been a recluse, also has her difficulties and has to learn to accept help from others. After a year without any contact with their mother, Dicey and her grandmother travel to the hospital where she is unconscious and dies.

This book could be very useful for a younger teenager who has to adjust to living in a new family, especially if she has been the oldest and has had to take a lot of responsibility.

Dodger

Libby Gleeson

Puffin Books (1992) new edition   0 140 036063 8   £4.95

Mick now in his early teens had been taken to live with his grandmother many years previously when his mother died. His father is a long distance truck driver and rarely visits them. Some of his mates are changing and developing new interests and Mick is lonely. He finds school work boring and the PE teacher picks on him. A young teacher arrives who makes her lessons interesting and she pays attention to him. She persuades Mick to take a lead part in the school musical. During rehearsals, he tentatively starts to make friends and with his teacher's help eventually starts to recall the traumatic time round the death of his mother. He had not been allowed to say good-bye, attend the funeral or to mourn her and has been suppressing guilt feelings about not preventing her death. He also desperately wants contact with his absent father. At times he is very angry. After successfully taking part in the school musical, and with some counselling help, he persuades his father to take him to his mother's grave for the first time.

This Australian novel may be useful for a boy in his early teens.

Emma says Goodbye

Carolyn Nystrom, Annabel Large

Lion Publications, 1993   0 7459 2759 9   £3.99

Emma and Auntie Sue make a quilt together after she has come to live with the family. They share happy memories and talk whilst working together. But Auntie Sue is struggling with cancer. She has chemotherapy and is getting thinner and thinner. The family adjusts to her getting progressively more ill. They ask God to help her get well; they sing hymns and read from the Bible. Auntie Sue has a period of feeling better and Emma hopes God wouldn't let her die, not if they keep asking him to make her well. The two of them continue to make the quilt. The cancer flares up again and X-rays damage her skin and she is more tired than ever. Emma gets depressed and is supported by her loving family. Auntie Sue says that "God hears our prayers. And I know that he loves us. But he doesn't always give us what we ask – even when it is as important as life." Emma feels angry with God. Auntie Sue dies with the family around her, reading the Bible and big brother playing the guitar until she has stopped breathing. Months after the funeral, the quilt is finished and Emma believes that 'somewhere, in greener grass, under bluer skies and lusher trees, Auntie Sue was tall and tanned and strong – dancing with Jesus'

This is a beautiful book with good illustrations and sensitive text. It is an excellent book that would be very helpful in a Christian environment for a more mature child of middle to upper primary school age.

Ewen's Little Brother
Sheila Lamont, Pauline Joyce
Victoria Publication, 1988
The Royal Victoria Infirmary, Queen Victoria Road,
Newcastle-on-Tyne NE1 4LP   1 871476 02 X   £1.75

Ewen had a little brother called Gavin. They loved to play together, they went shopping with Mum. Gavin became very ill and had to go to hospital for treatment. One day Gavin died. They went to his funeral and they knew he was in heaven and he was no longer ill and he did not need his body any more. Sometimes Ewen feels upset.

A colourful and useful picture book for nursery age children and those who have started school.

Facilitator Guide for Drawing out Feelings
Marge Heegaard
Woodland Press, 1992
99 Woodland Circle,
Minneapolis, MN 55424, USA   0 9620502 53

The facilitator's guide is written for those who intend to lead grief support groups. Children of primary school age up to pre-teenage can be helped either in groups or individually through the structured sessions with an adult. Through drawing, children can express feelings they cannot easily talk about or understand. There are three workbooks by this author, each to be covered in six sessions. The titles of the three workbooks can be found under the author's name in the alphabetical list.

This book for the facilitator is divided into three units: Helping Children Cope with Loss and Change, Structure for Children's Grief Support Group and Childhood Bereavement. The book then covers how each one of the workbooks for children can be used, what equipment is needed, and laying a clear plan of how to organise each session.

Facing Bereavement

Ed: Ann Warren

Highland Books, 1988	0 946616 36 1	Out of print

Each chapter is written by a committed Christian describing his or her personal experiences with the death of a family member and the subsequent struggles with their faith. There is a family whose new-born baby died, the loss of a toddler from a brain tumour, the loss of a young adult in a climbing accident as well as the loss of adult relatives. There is a chapter by a terminally ill doctor facing up to coping with his own dying and death.

This book could be very useful for an older teenager or adult Christian going through bereavement.

Facing Grief

Susan Wallbank

Bereavement and the Young Adult

Lutterworth Press, 1991	0 7188 2807 0	£6.95

Suffering a bereavement at an age when most are leaving home to start adult life is difficult, especially if you have to take on adult responsibilities for the practical arrangements. It deals in a clear way with the practicalities of what happens when someone dies. Information is given about funeral arrangements and legal issues as well as about feelings and grief work. There are helpful chapters dealing with the implications of the death of relatives as well as death in the new family that a young couple has created. Each page is split into small sub-headed paragraphs, making it easier to find the information that is applicable. There is practical advice as well as a list of helpful organisations and addresses. The author is a Cruse counsellor.

A book that is easy to read and aimed at the 18–28 age group and those around them.

Feelings
Aliki
Pan, 1987   0 330 29408 3   £3.99

A lovely comic style book about emotions and how they are expressed. Each page has a different story about feelings with small colourful drawings and text. It deals with happiness, anger, fear, jealousy, sadness, feeling good, loneliness, nervousness etc. There is one page with conversation between two children about feeling sad about the death of a pet mouse.

This is a really useful book to help children explore and name feelings but it does not deal with bereavement.

Finding out about Bereavement
Scottish Health Education Group
Woodburn House
Canaan Lane, Edinburgh EH10 4SG

A useful little twelve page pamphlet about feelings around bereavement with information on how bereaved people react, how friends can help, decisions about arrangements for the funeral and the costs involved. There is a small reference list of addresses and books. Written for adults.

Fred
Posy Simmonds
Picture Puffin (1987) new edition   0 14 050965 8   £3.99

Everybody was very sad to hear that Fred, the cat that lived with Nick and Sophie, had died. One night the children are woken up by a loud noise in the garden. When they sneak out, they discover that there is a huge funeral with all Fred's admirers attending followed by a party in the street.

This is a delightful book, funny and touching with pictures full of details that children will love to look at. It may not be a book to help a child dealing with personal bereavement but it is a cheerful book dealing with a painful topic. For older children of primary school age.

Gill and Mark, East Enders' Great Love Story

Susanna Dawson

Red Fox, 1993   0 09 931841 5   £3.50

A book of fictional extracts from the stories of the two young people in the TV series, EastEnders, who both found out that they were HIV infected. Gill died. Mixed with the romantic story of their meeting and falling in love is factual information about HIV, STDs, condom use, HIV testing and interviews with actual persons about HIV. There are some extracts from the TV script including Gill's death scene. There is an interview with a buddy, information from people living and working in a hospice on how to support someone who is ill and short notes on terminal illness. The book is illustrated with comic pen drawings as well as photographs from the TV series. There is a glossary and a list of helpful organisations.

The book is not written for someone close to HIV but is useful for teenagers who want to know more and pupils in a secondary school where HIV is an issue.

Going into Hospital

Althea

Dinosaur Publications, 1986   0 85122 539 X   £1.75

A small book with colourful drawings full of details of what happens in a children's ward. Lisa isn't well enough to eat with the other children so she has a tube inserted into her arm. Anna has blood taken from her finger. John has an X-ray. Ben came in an ambulance because he had a bad pain in his tummy. He has had an operation and uses a special potty. Sharon will have her tonsils out and Jas, an injection to make her feel sleepy. When she wakes up she feels a bit sick but later she is better and goes home. For pre-school children and just above, in age.

Going to Hospital

Camilla Jessel

Methuen Children's Books, 1983   0 416 25990 1   Out of print

There are colour photographs with a short text on the opposite pages in this small book written for very young children. Jamie is feeling ill and has to go to hospital where he is examined. He eats lunch in bed. He is wheezing and has a mask with air. Mum sleeps in a bed next to his cot. He plays with the other children and has an X-ray before taking his medicine and returning home.

A simple and reassuring book for pre-school children.

Going to the Hospital: First experiences
Anne Civardi, Stephen Cartwright
Usborne (1986) new edition   0 7460 1511 9   £2.50

Ben has earache and Dr Small says that he needs an operation. He is taken to the ward and is examined by the surgeon and is prepared for the operation. After the operation he feels better, there is visiting time and finally he goes home.

A simple picture book for very young children, between 3 and 5 years old.

Good Grief – Exploring feelings, loss and death with over 11s and adults
Barbara Ward and Associates
Good Grief, 19 Bawtree Road,
Uxbridge, Middlesex UB8 1PT, 1992   0 9512 888 53 0   £28.25

An excellent resource pack written for educators with contributions from a range of different professionals. Section Two contains activities with worksheets that are photocopiable. Section Three contains articles, book lists, both for students and adults, as well as useful addresses.

This book would be a valuable addition in a resource library for those with a pastoral responsibility for teenagers.

Good Grief – Exploring feelings, loss and death with under 11s
Barbara Ward and Associates
19 Bawtree Road, Uxbridge,
Middlesex UB8 1PT, 1988   0 9512888 2 2   £28.25

The book has been designed to provide a framework within a school for exploring feelings and issues round loss and death for children of different abilities under 12 years of age. It starts with the background to grief and mourning experienced by children, death of a family member and also from other losses from a variety of reasons including moving, the death of a pet, change of culture, having a new sibling, living with a handicap, and separation and divorce. There are contributions by a variety of authors with experience of working with children. The grief reactions that may occur in young children are covered. Although the book often provides suggestions for teachers much of the material is just as helpful for parents.

The second section contains a rich variety of creative activities that can be used with a child or a school class to work through grief and help identify feelings. There are also activities suggested to help develop self-esteem. Work done by children of different ages are included throughout to illustrate the kind of work children can produce.

The appendices contain additional information such as addresses and a book list.

This is an excellent resource, well written with short chapters easy to read. This is a book that would be useful in any primary school resource library and public libraries where parents and concerned adults can find it.

Goodbye and Keep Cold

Jenny Davies

Orchard Books, 1988   1 85213 071 7   £7.95

The story follows Edda from the time her father died until she leaves home in her late teens. Edda's young father was killed in a mining accident when she was 8 years old. Both she and her mother were devastated as their lives had seemed so happy. They live with baby Jimmy and an old uncle as a lodger and there is not much money about. Local people came to help and the house filled with strangers before the funeral. The man who caused the mining accident befriends Edda's mother and two years later he proposes to her. She cannot yet start a new relationship so the family is left on their own while she is still grieving for and worshipping the memory of her dead husband. Edda has difficulties in school and feels friendless. The family eventually moves away but some years later Edda's mother meets up with him again. They marry after some further complications and Edda leaves home to go to college.

For teenagers.

Goodbye Tomorrow

Gloria Miklowitz

Lions Teen Tracks, 1987   0 00 672913 4   Out of print

This story of 17 year-old Alex, his girlfriend, sister and family, is set in America in the early days of the AIDS epidemic. Alex became infected through a blood transfusion and develops ARC a year later. Alex tries to deal with the fact that he has tested HIV positive by himself but his changed behaviour affects all around him. He is scared that he might have infected his girlfriend and of being exposed to prejudice. Suspicion spreads in the school and friends withdraw. Relationships with his girlfriend, sister and parents change. When suspicion becomes too widespread, he has to stop attending school although this decision is finally overturned.

This book is not for someone affected by HIV because some facts are wrong: the rejection of Alex by those in authority would hopefully not happen today. This story could be scary for someone who feels vulnerable.

Grandpa's Slide Show

Deborah Gould

Picture Puffin, 1990   0 14 050871 6   Out of print

Whenever Sam and his brother stayed at their grandparents' house, Grandpa always had a slide show of family photos. The boys knew some of the people in the slides, but many were taken before they were born. One time when the boys came, there was no slide show because Grandpa was very ill. He died and the adults had to organise the funeral. After the funeral they had another slide show and saw a picture of Grandpa the way he was.

A moving picture story book about a loving family and the practical activities round a death. It is written for young children.

Granpa

John Burningham

Jonathan Cape, 1994   0 224 02279 2   £9.99

A large picture book without a printed story. There are big, colourful pictures, full of details, with one sentence on each double page spread. It is about a little girl and her Granpa and the things the two of them enjoy doing together. Towards the end of the book he is seen not to be well. On the second last page his chair is empty and there is no text at all. This is a book to be shared between a child and an adult where they can describe to each other what is happening in each picture.

There is a video of the book as well. For an adult to read with a young child of pre-school age and upwards.

Grief and AIDS

Ed: Lorraine Sherr

John Wiley and Sons, 1995   0 471 95346 6   £12.99

The authors of the different chapters are writing for professionals involved with counselling and supporting both adults and children. The contributors are from different countries affected by HIV and the editor has produced a book that reads well. The text explores many of the notions of grief related to AIDS and deals with those who are bereaved as they lose a parent, child, partner, lover or patient. Many of the bereaved are HIV positive themselves.

It is acknowledged that HIV infection affects not only those infected but also their wider families and those who are involved in their care and support. Loss is felt already when the person finds out about being HIV positive and from then on, a number of different losses have to be faced by the infected individual as well as those close to him or her. The issues round grief, in the context of AIDS, have additional aspects to those experienced by individuals and families facing other terminal conditions.

The book provides overviews on current thoughts in counselling and psychotherapeutic considerations as well as information on clinical practice. Each chapter refers to a wide range of written material including first hand experiences and has an extensive list of references at the end. The early chapters cover psychological aspects of grief in AIDS and HIV infection, the impact of the epidemic on the gay community in New York, and suicide and psychiatric problems associated with grief. There is a moving chapter written about Uganda where the infection rate ranges from 20 to 30 per cent of young urban adults. One author deals with the stress experienced by staff and carers that can lead to burnout. Another chapter deals with allowing someone to die, and living wills. For the purpose of this publication, the chapters on the death of a parent and the death of a child are particularly relevant.

The book aims to enable the reader to become aware of many facets of grief, on the assumption that insight and understanding may lighten the load. This is a helpful and thought-provoking book for professionals.

Grief, Bereavement and Change – A quick guide
Penny Casdagli, Francis Gobey

Daniels, 1993   1 85467 307 6   £7.00

A small book of 53 pages to help schools develop aspects of the curriculum which play an important part in helping young people think about death. It is written by a Head Teacher who also chairs the National Association for Pastoral Care in Education.

The aim of the book is to define grief in relation to concepts such as loss, bereavement, and separation. This is a taboo subject, yet one that is constantly on TV both in films and news programmes. The growth of the hospice movement and AIDS has also increased the awareness of death amongst school-aged children. Schools are beginning to approach the issue of grief either through whole-school policies or the taught curriculum, often because of a death or a crisis affecting the school community.

The book suggests how a school community can prepare for events which can bring grief responses in children. The National Curriculum promotes a whole-school approach combining pastoral care and the health curriculum. The book covers the effects, stages, feelings and processes of grieving. The bereaved young person can regard the school as an island of respite from the mourning environment but may also display disruptive behaviour, truancy and denial. The book also touches on the possible effects of grief on the family, factors affecting young people in bereaved families, and how to support them. There is information on planning a course and suitable resources and books are suggested.

A very useful book for school management and teachers responsible for the pastoral care in a school.

Grief in Children – A handbook for adults
Atle Dyregrov
Jessica Kingsley, 1991   1 85302 113 X   £12.95

The book is aimed at adults to help them understand how to respond appropriately to the needs of a bereaved child. It explains how children of different ages understand death and how adults can best help them cope. It deals with physical and psychological reactions and describes methods that have been shown to work well in different situations. There is advice for counsellors and teachers as well as for parents. There are clear guidelines for caring for individual children as well as an excellent chapter on how to handle death with a play group and at school. There is also a chapter on the need for adults to care for themselves when working with a bereaved child.

This book is liked by adults working with bereaved children and is highly recommended to all people training to work with children in a professional capacity as well as management staff planning a school's response to the needs of bereaved children.

Helping Children Cope with Grief – Facing a death in the family
Rosemary Wells
Sheldon Press, 1988   0 85969 559 X   £5.99

This is an excellent book for adults who want to help a child through bereavement and loss, either as a parent, social worker, counsellor or caring adult. There are examples of children losing parents through death or divorce or through disrupted foster placements. The author gives practical suggestions on how to tell a child, from a very young child to a teenager, about the death of a parent or loss of the family. There are examples of how children show or repress feelings of sadness, anger and guilt, followed by ways of opening up a discussion through exercises. There is also very practical advice about how to make the child feel cherished such as the importance of a cuddly blanket as well as various activities to help a young child deal with feelings. She illustrates the 'magical thinking' common to so many children, 'If I am really good, Daddy will come back', and shows how some understanding of what is going on in the mind of the bereaved child is a first step towards helping him or her sort out the pain, confusion and guilt. There are suggestions on how to help improve a child's sense of self-esteem and how to improve relationships between parents and children. The book stresses the importance of being honest with children, and on being explicit in a way that is comprehensible to a child. The author, a child therapist, obviously has a lot of personal experience of helping children and she comes across as a warm, sensitive and caring person.

This could be an essential book for an adult who wants to help a child through bereavement and loss. It is particularly suitable for someone in training for working with children.

A book liked by adults working with children.

Helping Children Cope with Separation and Loss – Child care policy and practice

Claudia Jewett

B T Batsford Ltd, London, 1994
Revised second edition   0 7134 7766 0   £13.99

A book written for an adult who wants to help a grieving child. The book offers practical advice on how to help a child through the recovery process. This is underpinned by theory to clarify the issues for the reader and make it easier to respond to the child. It describes behaviour patterns that can be expected immediately after the loss and those that may appear many years later. The author is a child and family therapist working at the North American Centre for Adoption. The book is published in association with the British Agencies for Adopting and Fostering.

The first section deals with how and when to tell the child about the loss, what to do first and how to help make the adjustment easier for the child. Loss is suffered not only through death but also through separation and divorce, and other changes in the family. The second section deals with helping children face such changes. This is followed by some chapters on the normal progression through grief, and how to support grief work, helping children cope with strong emotions such as anger, aggression and also sadness. The author deals with how to identify and help a child, who seems to be stuck in the grief work, to move forward. The book ends with how to let go and move on.

The frequent examples and dialogues, together with techniques and descriptions of simple methods to enable a child to communicate and express feelings, makes this a very helpful book indeed.

HIV and AIDS in Children: A guide for the family

Rebekah Lwin, Candy Duggan, Diana Gibb

The Hospitals for Sick Children and
the Institute of Child Health, 1993   1 898081 10 7   £2.50

This is an information leaflet for parents of infected children dealing with infection, keeping well, how to prepare the child for coming to hospital, what happens at the Outpatients Clinic and ' Who can I talk to?' There is a good glossary and a list of addresses.

A useful booklet for adults.

HIV/AIDS and Sex – Information for young people

AVERT

11–13 Denne Parade, Horsham,
West Sussex RH12 1DJ 1994   £3.50 for 10

A booklet of 18 pages aimed at young adults, and concentrating on sexual transmission of HIV. The information is given in a clear, matter of fact way and emphasises the use of condoms. The booklet recognises that young people have differing views about sex and makes it clear that no-one should be pressured into having sex when they would rather not. An excellent book to hand to teenagers before they start being sexually active. For mid-teens.

HIV/AIDS – Telling the children

Barnardo's

Daniels Publishing, 1992   0 902046 11X   £38

This is the result of a one day conference held in 1992 and consists of articles written for teachers by different professionals concerned that young teenagers should have the right to know about HIV and AIDS. It deals with different strategies for teaching HIV and sex education within the curriculum in England and Wales including working with younger children and the use of drama. A mother writes about her HIV positive daughter's experience at school. Issues for parents and carers are introduced. The issues round sex education with children from multi-faith backgrounds are also touched on. There is information on the Dutch perspective on health education.

This is an introduction for teachers to some of the issues.

HIV/AIDS and the Under Fives: A guide for workers and carers

Ed: Ronno Griffiths

Manchester AIDSline Women's Group, 1991
PO Box 201, Manchester M60 1PU   £5.00

This A4 booklet was written and collated by volunteers involved in the care of young children. It reflects the concerns of nursery staff, social services and those concerned with fostering and adoption. Although starting off with factual information on HIV and AIDS, the book focuses on helping the reader explore attitudes to HIV and those infected and affected, and issues round confidentiality. There is a chapter on good practice in hygiene followed by how to deal with childhood illnesses, vaccines and infections. It explores the fact that children may have special needs either as infected or affected by parental illness. The health care services available are outlined as well as that of social services and housing. The question of the needs of carers are acknowledged.

This is a booklet of only 35 pages, easy to read and reassuring for those working with young children.

HIV Infection and Children in Need

Ed: Daphne Batty

British Agencies for Adoption and Fostering, 1993
11 Southwark Street, London, SE1 1RQ   1 873868 08 1   £9.99

A collection of articles written by different contributors for those planning services and for professionals working with children affected by HIV/AIDS. It contains articles on transmission, sero-positive babies, caring for children and families infected and affected by HIV, planning for children affected by AIDS, issues for those developing services for families from ethnic groups, coping with bereavement, adopting infected children and living with HIV positive people. The chapter dealing with legal issues refers to English law. There is a bibliography and addresses of useful organisations.

A very useful book for adults.

Hospital

John Colerne, Chris Fairclough

Franklin Watts, 1987   0 86313 611 7   Out of print

A hardback book with a couple of simple sentences on each page and colour photographs showing what goes on in a hospital. There are photographs of both children and adult patients, some nursing procedures, the play room, laboratory, hospital kitchen, etc.

A reassuring book for young children which could be used with children with special educational needs as well.

How Can I Tell You?

Mary Tasker

Association for the Care of Children's Health,
Bethesda, Maryland USA, 1992   0 937821 82 9   £12.95

The author has worked with HIV infected children and their families. This book deals with issues around disclosing their HIV diagnosis to children. The author believes that children should be told but not without the consent and participation of their parents. Despite all the obstacles to telling, many parents eventually decide to disclose the diagnosis and the majority feel a great sense of relief when this is done. Short case stories illustrate the points she wants to make.

The chapters explore the reasons why parents don't want to tell the infected child, the burden of secrecy, the stigma and discrimination acting as barriers to disclosure, and how to cope with these. She goes on to deal with what she calls the four phases of disclosure.

This is a very useful book for professionals wanting to help parents work out how to tell their child about their HIV infection.

How it Feels to Fight for your Life

Jill Krementz

Victor Gollancz, 1990   0 575 04770 4   Out of print

Fourteen children aged between 7 and 16 tell their stories about fighting for their lives. They cover conditions such as spina bifida, leukaemia, asthma, aplastic anaemia, lupus, cystic fibrosis, osteogenic sarcoma, etc. Each child's story is illustrated with several photographs. The experiences they describe deal with painful treatments in hospital, their suffering and anxieties, how their families and friends are reacting, but also the support they have received from other children and medical staff in hospital, and their wish to fight for life.

It is a good book for older primary age children and young teenagers undergoing chemotherapy and difficult medical procedures.

How it Feels when a Parent Dies

Jill Krementz

Victor Gollancz, 1983   0 575 03290 1   Out of print

This book consists of interviews and photographs of 18 children aged, 7–15, who have lost a parent. The children are American and come from different races and backgrounds. The deaths they have experienced include death by accident, illness, and suicide. Each young person describes what it felt like when they were told about the death and what has happened afterwards, both to their lives and how they adjusted to their loss. Some describe their feelings about their parent getting a new partner. They describe their memories and how it feels now. Some visit graveyards where their parent is buried.

The personal accounts are very readable as if spoken by the children themselves. Their stories are immediate and realistic. A bereaved child may find some of his or her own experiences mirroring that of one of the children in the book. A very useful book for 9–14 year-olds.

I Heard the Owl call my Name

Margaret Craven

Heinemann (1978) new editon   0 435 12229 0   £4.75

A young Anglican priest with an undisclosed terminal condition is sent to work in an Indian village in British Columbia. While working and living with the villagers, he learns about life, and when he hears the owl call his name, he realises that he will die soon and now he can accept it.

A very moving story, well written and with insight, and is suitable to be read by older teenagers.

I Never Told Her I Loved Her

Sandra Chick

The Women's Press, 1989   0 7043 4912 4   £2.95

Frankie's mother is dead and she lives on a farm with her father who suddenly seems to have aged. She feels totally lost, angry, guilty and hurt. Her present life is mixed up with memories of her mother, some good ones and others, irritating and negative. Life seems to go on around her yet she cannot participate – she is thinking of her Mum and the past, the whole time. She is trying to work out whether her parents' marriage was the good one that her father refers to. She remembers how they shouted at each other at times.

Frankie is in an angry stage of her grief and this book may not be of use to someone who is in a different stage of grieving. It is a very realistic portrait of a family where the parents were doing their best but where they did not seem to have much in common. Frankie was and is not an easy teenager.

A book for teenagers.

I'll Always Love You

Hans Wilhelm

Hodder and Stoughton, 1992   0 340 40153 2   £3.95

A picture book about Elfie, the best dog in the world, and a boy. They play together, Elfie gets into mischief but is loved even while scolded. Elfie grew older, became rounder, slept more and didn't want to walk outdoors. The boy carried him upstairs to bed – he was still loved. One morning Elfie was dead and got buried. All in the family cried but the boy remembered that he had told Elfie 'I'll always love you'. Some day he would have another dog or a kitten.

Nice clear pictures. To be read with a young child, introducing death with old age.

Inside a Hospital

Gillian Mercer

Kingfisher Books, 1988   0 86272 360 4   Out of print

The book is full of colourful, detailed drawings of all the different professionals who work in a hospital, what the different rooms are called and what goes on in a children's ward before and after an operation. Amy has a hernia and has been admitted for an operation. She undergoes a number of procedures and each is illustrated. There are other children on the ward who are having different treatments such as a girl in traction. Pieces of medical equipment are drawn and named. The routine on the ward is explained in drawings and text. Mum stays the night. The hospital at night is drawn with activities going on in the maternity unit and the Accident and Emergency Department. Next morning Amy is prepared for her operation and is brought there with her Mum. The staff in the operating theatre are named. Amy wakes up on the ward and goes home two days later. Joe fell off a climbing frame and has to have an X-ray and gets a dressing put on.

The book is prepared by the National Association for the Welfare of Children in Hospital.

It is interesting book for a pre-school or primary age child and suitable for a child who is to have an operation.

It's Clinic Day

Ruth Stevens, Fiona Menzies

Health Promotion Department,
61 Grange Loan Edinburgh EH9 2ER   0 9519341 0 4

This book was written by a HIV positive mother who saw the need for a book to help parents talk with their child about going to the clinic for a regular check up and having tests done. There are other children in the waiting room, some with HIV and AIDS. Jane is examined and the doctor explains that she has white blood cells that chase bugs away. The doctor does not know whether Jane has HIV but she is fine and well now. The doctor tells Jane about all the ways HIV cannot be caught.

The illustrations on each page are colourful and the visit to the clinic is dealt with light-heartedly and aims to be reassuring. For young children.

Jimmy and the Egg Virus

Mary Tasker

Children's Hospital AIDS Program, 1988
Children's Hospital of New Jersey, United Hospitals Medical Centre
15 South Ninth Street , Newark, New Jersey 07107

A soft picture book with simple line drawings in black, white and blue of three children who attend the clinic at the hospital. They tell the reader with speech bubbles about the HIV or AIDS virus. Jimmy overheard his Mom talk about an 'egg' virus with Grandma and got really mixed up until the doctor at the hospital put him right. Dr Linda goes on to talk about HIV and AIDS and what is happening in the blood.

The text is simple yet covers a lot that a young child may want to know. On the last page Mom says 'Jimmy, the AIDS virus scares all of us. But you're right, it helps when we talk to each other about how we feel.'

An important book for primary age children living with HIV.

John's Book

Jill Fuller, Bill Toop

The Lutterworth Press, 1993
PO Box 60, Cambridge CB1 2NT   0 7188 2870 4   £9.99

John's father died very suddenly leaving him and his mother to deal with a range of problems and emotions. John is between 10 and 13 years of age. During the time between the death and the funeral, John stays with relatives. His two young cousins have to face this death as well. Immediately after the funeral all actions feel like a film in slow motion. One day when angry, he throws stones through the glass panes of the family green house until a neighbour stops him. The man helps him repair it and talks about his own previous bereavement.

Mum and John struggle on, adjusting to their changed life. Panic fears for the safety of his mother make John stop going to school until he is discovered and helped by his teacher to talk about his feelings.

A little girl living nearby has lost her mother, and with her father starts to join John and his mother. Eventually John's mother tells him that she would like to marry this widower. John and his mother have to adjust to yet another change which leads to the creation of a new family.

This is a sensitive and useful book for any child who has lost a parent and has to find courage to 'trust life again'.

The author has first hand experience of bereaved children and how they have to learn to meet their friends again, accept their loss and face their future. For older primary age children.

Just Like Me
Positive Action
Somerset Health Authority
Wellspring Road, Taunton TA2 7PQ

Pen drawings of 'my best friend Lee' who has HIV in his blood. Sometimes he is ill, at other times he is well; the two children play together and they like the same things. The text is simple and repetitive. A book to read with a very young child affected by HIV.

Listen, my child has a lot of living to do: Caring for children with life-threatening conditions
Ed: J D Baum, Sr Frances Dominica, R N Woodward
Oxford University Press, 1990	0 19 261961 6	£7.50
British Agencies for Adoption and Fostering, 1993		
11 Southwark Street, London SE1 1RQ	1 873868 08 1	£9.99

This is a collection of articles written by professionals about their involvement with afflicted children and families. A GP writes both as a father and in his professional capacity, another man whose child had cancer describes how a trust for terminally ill children and their families grew from their needs. The experiences gained in different children's hospices, hospital based services as well as domiciliary nursing care and their aims are described. There are personal accounts both from parents, the children and the professional carers. It touches on the burden of unrelenting and progressive illness, the threat of premature death and the need for spiritual, emotional and physical support that is common to all. The contributions represent the experiences both of families and their expert views on how services could be improved in the future as well as that of the service providers. This is a book for those wanting to improve or develop provisions for children with life threatening conditions. There is an extensive address list of organisations and services for terminally ill children in Britain.

Living with AIDS in the Community
WHO

WHO Global Programme on AIDS,
Geneva, Switzerland, 1992

A thin booklet written and produced in the Republic of Uganda. The pages are full of pen drawings and text of family and village situations in Uganda. The aim is to help people make the best of the situations around AIDS. There is information about transmission, about feelings when you find out that you are infected, about living positively with HIV and AIDS, and how to care for yourself and those close to you.

This book may be useful for a teenager or adult from an African background. It may be available in other languages; WHO keeps a record of translations. The book is copyright free.

Losing Uncle Tim
Mary Kate Jordan, Judith Friedman

Albert Whiteman and Co, 1989   0 8075 4756 5   Out of print

Uncle Tim had an antique store and it was great fun for the young boy to be with him. They did a lot of nice things together. One day Uncle Tim fell asleep while talking. Mom said that Uncle Tim's body was getting worn out from a disease called AIDS. The next time they met, he looked different to the boy as he now knew about AIDS. Uncle Tim got more tired and his appearance changed as time went on. The boy was very distressed and was comforted by his parents. He was also afraid of catching AIDS himself. Uncle Tim was in a coma the last time the boy visited him and then he died. Everybody went to the funeral. The boy got a favourite toy that had been Uncle Tim's. Each time he sees the toy on his desk it brings back memories.

A beautifully illustrated book with a supportive and sensitive text for young and older primary age children. An excellent book.

Loss and Change

Peter Marris

Routledge (1986) new edition   0 415 09862 9   £11.99

Peter Marris is a social scientist who shows how understanding grief can help us understand other changes, both social and in society. Grieving is a way of working out a psychological re-integration when life falls apart. He draws on a variety of studies both in Britain and abroad. There are chapters on bereavement, slum clearance, tribalism, mourning and the management of change. A book written for adults with an interest in sociology.

Mary and her Grandmother

Bettina Egger

Viking Kestrel, 1987   0 670 81746 5   Out of print

When Mary's grandmother dies, Mary remembers all the things that she had shared with Granny. Mary comes to realise that she still loves her grandmother even though she knows that she won't see her again.

A large picture book with attractive whole page illustrations. A book to read together with a young child to talk about death and shared good memories.

Maybe Another Day

Fiona Mitchell, Mark Mackenzie-Smith

Paediatric AIDS Resource Centre, 1995
20 Sylvan Place, Edinburgh EH9 1UW   1 900339 00 5   £2.50

Lucy and her mum love to play in the park and go swimming together. Sometimes her mother gets tired and sick and they can't do the things they enjoy. "Maybe another day" replies Mum. Lucy feels angry and sad. At other times Mum feels fine again.

There are blank pages for the child to draw what he or she enjoys, the feelings when Mum is sick, and how he or she feels when happy.

The cartoon illustrations are bright and cheerful.

This book will be followed by further books *Missing Mum* when she is in hospital, about going into foster care and finally about bereavement when Mum dies. The cause of Mum's illness is not mentioned.

This is a small interactive booklet to be read with a young child of pre-school or early primary school age together with an adult who will encourage the child to draw in on the clear pages.

Me and My Mates

Aidan MacFarlane, Ann McPherson

Pan Books, 1991   0 330 32615 X   £2.99

Each member of a group of teenage friends who want to 'be on the scene' tells their story of the events that led up to a disastrous party. They are all aware of HIV.

Written by two doctors who researched the book using friends, teenagers, *Just Seventeen* and journals. A book written to warn teenagers about HIV.

Illustrated with comic drawings and written for young teenagers.

Meggie's Magic

Anna Dean, Colin Stephens

Kestrel Picture Books, 1992   0 670 82761 4   £8.99

'When Meggie was eight years old she got very sick and died. Now there's just Mummy, Daddy and me'. A sensitive story about a family coming to terms with grief. It is about the memories from the secret place that the two sisters used to share, now tucked away inside the little sister and how Meggie's magic is still there in the memories of all the family members.

The pictures are bold and bright and the story is written by someone who understands how young children cope with grief.

Thoroughly recommended for young children.

Memory

Margaret Mahy

Penguin (1988) new edition   0 14 032680 4   £4.50

Jonny is an angry, confused older teenager at odds with the world. His sister died five years earlier. In his alienation he gets befriended by a helpless old woman with senile dementia who lives in dreadful squalor. Jonny starts to care for the old woman and through what happens, both their lives change. The death of his sister is only incidental but the pain and alienation from unresolved grief may be recognised by a teenager a year or so after their own bereavement.

Mummy goes into Hospital

Evelyn Elliot, Christopher Cormack

Hamish Hamilton, 1985   0 241 11475 6   £5.50

A small hardback book with large colour photographs of a family with three children. One day Mummy tells the family that she is going into hospital for a few days to have an operation. We follow the family packing her suitcase, going with her to hospital and settling into the ward. The children and Daddy visit her after the operation when she has a drip. There are photographs of the family getting on with everyday activities at home and visiting Mummy as she gets stronger. Eventually they all collect Mummy who has to walk slowly – they cannot sit in her lap when she reads them a story at home; however, she will soon be able to take the children to the zoo.

A reassuring book for children of pre-school and early primary school age.

My Mum Needs Me: Helping children with ill or disabled parents

Julia Segal, John Simkins

Penguin, 1993   0 14 016652 1   £6.99

The book deals with the pressures placed on children when a parent falls ill or becomes disabled. The book is the result of research, counselling and personal experience over many years. It is written for parents, friends, teachers, therapists and social workers involved with children in families where a parent is ill. The book contains suggestions on how to talk with children about these difficult issues and suggest ways in which an ill parent can help their children themselves.

This is a very helpful book.

Night Kites

M E Kerr

Pan Horizon, 1987   0 330 30061 X   Out of print

Two 17 year-old American boys seem to have the usual worries about relationships with girl friends and parents until the older brother of one of them discloses that he has AIDS. The family members did not know he was gay. They have to adjust to the fact that their perception of being a happy normal family is no longer true. The older brother comes home to live as he loses his flat and job. The family is shunned.

The characters and their stories are not entirely engaging. For teenagers.

Not a Worry in the World

Marcia Williams

Walker Books, 1990   0 7445 1539 4   £6.99

A big picture book full of tiny delightful details that are about all the worries Alfie has. Both adults and children will recognise many of them. On the last page when Alfie has found out the secret of worries, all his worries run away.

This is a lovely book. It may be very useful for a child who has worries about what is going on at home and a useful way to let the child identify his or her own worries together with an adult. For primary age children.

On Children and Death

Elisabeth Kübler-Ross

Macmillan 1985   0 02 089144 X   £6.95

This is a very personal book written by a doctor who has now written eight books on death and dying and run workshops all over the world for those who are bereaved and grieving. This book is based on her experience over a decade with dying children and from her work with parents and siblings. The book includes many letters and personal accounts from family members who have lost a child under different circumstances as well as from children themselves – toddlers to teenagers. The aim is to enable us as adults to help each other, the dying child and the siblings. The author firmly believes that dying children often know death far beyond the comprehension of adults and their inner spiritual intuition can teach adults about death. The book starts with a letter to parents who are in the process of losing a child and deals with the issues both of the dying child as well as the needs of the parents and the siblings. The author is, at times, quite critical of the lack of understanding displayed by professionals to the needs both of the dying child and of the grieving family members.

There are chapters on the natural way to prepare children for life and death, loss as a catalyst for growth and understanding, murdered children and childhood suicide as well as the use of visualisation as an alternative treatment. Spiritual aspects of the work with dying children are based on her vast experience of people of different ages sharing their near-death experiences, including a child of two who talked with his grandfather at the time of the old man's death, 18 miles away, and children clearly knowing when they are going to die or having had premonitions.

Hopefully, some of the mistakes described made through ignorance by professionals are less likely to happen today. This compassionate book could be supportive to parents.

One Green Leaf

Jean Ure

Corgi Freeway, 1990   0 552 52506 5   £2.25

Robyn and three others became friends when they started secondary school together. Later the wonderful and talented David becomes seriously ill with bone cancer. The feelings of David and his girl friend Abby are slowly perceived by Robyn as well as her own confused feelings when facing death for the first time. The feelings round serious illness are dealt with rather remotely and David's reactions are only vaguely touched on. The book might be helpful to the friends of a teenager with a terminal illness.

Parents and Teenagers – Understanding and improving communication about HIV/AIDS

Jo Frankham

AVERT, 1993   0 9515351 7 X   £3.00

This study found that many parents and teenagers wanted to be more open with each other but that there were many obstacles. It deals with parents as sex and AIDS educators as well as the views of teenagers. There is also a contribution from some Muslim parents. A short report for professionals planning HIV/AIDS and sex education.

Phoenix Rising or How to Survive your Life
Cynthia Grant

Lions Tracks, 1991   0 00 673732 3   Out of print

Jessie's older sister, Helen, died a few months ago of cancer which she had been fighting for some time. Jessie is about 16 years old. Life has changed completely for the whole family. Father and older brother argue and fight all the time, Mother is losing weight, Jessie is suffering terrible nightmares. She finds the diary her sister wrote in her last year and she can follow her sister's feelings as she became progressively more ill, undergoing chemotherapy, getting more and more tired and how her feelings changed. Jessie withdraws more and more from life into depression, fear of death and panic attacks until her family fears that they might lose her too. She cannot accept the help offered from a counsellor. With time, those around her manage to make contact with her, and she starts to change.

This could be a very helpful book for a teenager.

Reading Therapy for Children: A bibliography for hospital and home
Ed: Elizabeth Schlenther

Library Associations, 1992   0 9519452 0 3   Out of print
Next ed: Anne Brimlow, Southend Library
Victoria Avenue, Southend-on-Sea, SS26 6EX

This is an A4 publication with reviews of books suitable to be read with and for older children to read themselves as part of reading therapy. It lists books dealing with a particular disease, disability or emotional problem. The aims are similar to the aims of this bibliography – to gain information and to enable affected children to identify the feelings they share with a fictional character in a book or to disagree with the story line. The publication covers a variety of health problems such as cancer, cystic fibrosis and other life limiting conditions as well as family relationships, fear, anger, death and dying. A new edition is planned for the end of 1995 from the Health Libraries Group.

This is an extensive resource for adults.

Red Sky in the Morning

Elizabeth Laird

Piper Books (1988) new edition   0 330 30890 4   £3.50

Anna, who is 12 years old, has a baby brother, Ben, who is born badly handicapped. Anna develops a deep love for him. Fears of social isolation if others were to find out him not being perfect affect both Anna and her mother. The stress of looking after Ben day and night makes her mother exhausted and family members all suffer strain at home; Anna and her sister sometimes feel ignored. Anna slowly discovers that some people can actually share her love for Ben. She also has to grow up as a teenager and learn about relationships between the others in her class at school and she falls in love. When Ben is two years old, he suddenly dies. The family starts to come to terms with their tragedy and Anna discovers that she can use what she has learnt and help look after another handicapped child. She has matured over these few years and understands more about the feelings of others.

This is a well written and deeply moving story that is highly recommended for an older sibling of a child who is different from what was expected, or whose sibling has died. An older primary age child and young teenager might find this book very helpful.

Remembering Mum

Ginny Perkins, Leon Morris

A C Black, London, 1991   0 7136 3381 6   £5.95

Two small boys and their Dad helped to make this book in memory of their Mum who died the previous year. This is a book with photographs of the two boys throughout one day in an infant school with text describing the various things that happen such as getting hugs when sad in school, looking at the flowers planted in Mum's memory, visiting the grave, Dad crying, looking at photographs and sharing good memories, cooking and eating dinner together and finally having a bedtime story.

This picture book is to read with a young bereaved child showing familiar everyday scenes.

Risky Times – How to be AIDS-smart and stay healthy
Vincent Blake
Workman Publishing Co, US, 1990   0 89480 656 4   £4.99

An American book for teenagers where factual input is mixed with case stories of people in their early 20s living with AIDS, contracted through sex or needle sharing, and there is also a haemophiliac boy infected through blood products. There are many photographs and quotes and the book is very easy to read.

Younger teenagers would find this accessible, especially with all the personal stories.

Safer Sex – what you can do to avoid AIDS
Earvin Magic Johnson
Arrow Books, 1992   0 09 920021 X   Out of print

Written with the advice of doctors and experts to educate teenagers. The book starts with a chapter to parents. It then talks frankly about transmission routes of HIV and puts emphasis on being sexually responsible and delaying having sex, and it gives details of what safer sex means. It also covers other sexually transmitted diseases and the influence of alcohol and drugs on decision making. Finally there is advice on how to support someone who is HIV infected.

Although the book was originally American, it has been adapted for the British market and the resource list of addresses is all British.

This book could be very useful for senior pupils if kept in a school library.

Say Goodnight, Gracie
Julie Reece Deaver
Macmillan, 1989   0 333 47609 3   £3.99

Morgan and Jimmy have been best friends since they were born. They are 17 and are both developing their skills in order to become professional performing artists, taking classes, going to auditions, sharing jokes and supporting each other. Their mothers are best friends and their lives are comfortable and happy. When Jimmy is killed in a traffic accident Morgan's life is drastically changed. She refuses to take advice from either her parents or her young aunt who is a psychiatrist. It is only with time that she comes to realise that accepting help is okay, and that she has to let go of Jimmy and get on with her own life.

A well written book dealing with the pleasures of a close friendship that is suddenly shattered and replaced by anguish, sadness and loneliness. For teenagers.

Selina's Story

Jan Kalinski, David Potter

Barnardo's, 1995
Tanners Lane, Barkingside, Ilford, Essex IG6 1QG

This is Selina's story. She is a girl of primary age who has friends and goes to school. Her mother is sometimes ill because she has HIV. Grandad comes to take her to school and when Mummy has to be in hospital, Grandad stays over. Selina and her Mummy make a special book of memories for Selina to keep when Mummy dies. It won't be the same without Mummy but Selina will be looked after by her Grandad.

The text is simple and written for a young child about a very painful subject. The focus is on Selina's life now and the preparation for her future life without her mother, not about HIV. The drawings are in black and white and may appear to be for a child older than the text. This small book is written for children between 4 and 8 years of age.

Sirus the Virus

Somerset Health Authority

Wellsprings Road, Taunton, TA2 7PQ   £1.00

This is a six page A4 information cartoon aimed at giving information about HIV transmission and what happens in the body. It shows how viruses want to invade and attack the human body but there are barriers and an immune system to protect it. However, Sirus the Virus can attack the T cells which are part of the immune system and alter the programme of the cell. The body is in real trouble and doesn't know it. The virus cannot move to another body by being sneezed, or in tears or through kissing but the green spiky Sirus the Virus and its friends can travel in blood and through cuts. Sirus the Virus is happy if people share needles. On the last page some activities are drawn through which HIV cannot spread.

The spiky green viruses look aggressive. Sex is not mentioned. The cartoon could be used with children between 10 and 12, but not for anyone affected or infected with HIV.

Some of the Pieces
Melissa Madenski
Little, Brown and Co, 1991   0 316 54324 1   £7.99

A picture story about a family recovering a year after the death of Dylan's Dad. The family shares their memories of him. Their feelings of disbelief, anger, sadness and pain of missing Dad have gradually lessened until their thoughts of him can now make them smile together.

This is a book about death and healing – family members have suffered but there is a point when life begins to feel worth living again. The story is set in rural America and the pictures are beautiful. A really lovely book on how the family acknowledges their feelings and grows through their bereavement.

Thoroughly recommended for younger primary age children.

Someone Special has Died
Caroline Crossland
Dept. of Social Work, 1989
St Christopher's Hospice
51–59 Lawrie Park Road, London SE26 6DZ   0 16778 9252   £1.00

'When something so sad happens, we hope it isn't true, or we want to pretend it hasn't happened' starts this helpful book. It goes on to deal with how we feel, that it can take more than a year to get over so much sadness, that it might be hard to concentrate at school, that talking helps and how to remember. This is an excellent small book of only 8 pages with monochrome illustrations on each page using simple, straightforward language.

For younger children of primary school age.

Straight Talk about Death for Teenagers – How to cope with losing someone you love

Earl Grollman

Beacon Press, US, 1993   0 8070 2500 3   £6.99

The book is dedicated to bereaved teenagers to help them understand their emotions and manage their grief more wisely, and to discover that, although someone you love has died, you still want to go on living. The author explains what to expect when you lose someone you love, the feelings you may have and how grief can affect relationships with family and friends. It deals with how participating in a funeral can help and how to survive birthdays and anniversaries. The writing is well laid out with only a few paragraphs on each page, like poetry.

This is a book to give a recently bereaved teenager to read. It would be a very useful book for secondary school libraries.

Talkabout – Going into Hospital

Pauline Wells

Ladybird Books, 1985   0 7214 0849 4   Out of print

The book has realistic and detailed drawings with labels of the people a child would see in hospital, the reception area, the examination room and of various medical procedures. It has drawings of the ward and what happens there during the day.

There is only one sentence or a question on each page so that the child can fully explore what he or she can see. There are some sentences in small print with information for the parent. At the back of the book are a couple of pages with information for the parent to help him or her make the hospital stay easier for the child and themselves. For 3–7 year olds.

Talking about Bereavement

Scottish Health Education Group

Woodburn House
Canaan Lane, Edinburgh EH10 4SG   1 873452 42 X

An eight page leaflet on the grief process, helping ourselves and getting help from others, followed by some addresses and a short reading list. For adults.

Talking to Children when an Adult has Cancer
Cancerlink

Cancerlink, 1993

17 Britannia Street, London, WC1X 9JN   1 870534 34 4   £1.75

A small booklet of 35 pages that takes the view that it is helpful for everyone if children are involved in the events affecting the family when someone they live with has cancer. The short chapters of one page cover topics such as whether children should be told, how and what to tell them. It deals with how children react to illness and the sort of questions children are likely to ask, when to tell the school and friends and the need for planning ahead. It also deals with talking about dying and how to plan for the moment of death. This is a useful book for adults helping a child cope with a terminal illness in the family.

There is a list of organisations at the back.

Teens with AIDS Speak Out
Mary Kittredge

Julian Messner, US, 1991   0 671 74543 3   Out of print

Written by an author combining quotes and personal stories of young people with HIV/AIDS mixed with information about HIV transmission, testing, symptoms and treatments. It is not, as the title may suggest, interviews with or autobiographical notes written by the teenagers themselves. The term AIDS is used to cover both HIV and AIDS.

It is an American book written for teenagers with an educational purpose. This book could be used by teenagers doing a project on AIDS, looking for factual information and some personal anecdotes. There is a glossary. The list of helpful organisations contains only American addresses. Some teenagers may find the book patronising.

The Bereaved Parent
Harriet Sarnoff Schiff

Souvenir Press, 1979   0 285 64891 8   £7.99

The theme of the book is – the worst has happened to you. Nothing worse can happen. Feelings of grief, guilt and hopelessness, panic, sleeplessness and despair are dealt with. This is a helpful book written from personal experience by a mother whose 10 year-old son has died. It is written for bereaved parents with the reassuring message that there is hope, that as grieving parents you can survive. The book contains contributions by other grieving parents.

The Bumblebee Flies Anyway

Robert Cormier

Fontana Lions, 1983   0 00 672358 6   £3.50

This is an extraordinary book, one unlikely to be forgotten. The story is set in an experimental hospital ward where a few terminally ill teenage boys are undergoing treatment and in the story some of them die. The adult staff are perceived to be faceless, impersonal and uncomprehending of the psychological needs of the teenagers because it is difficult for adults to face the experience of the youngsters in a place like this. The seriously ill boys need each other's friendship and as much independence as their conditions allow. One day Barney has a vision and he evolves a crazy, daring plan that they carry out against all odds.

This is a book about pain and suffering and the strength of the human spirit and how human friendship can overcome immeasurable obstacles. The story is harsh and the descriptions of the terminal conditions are not pleasant.

Before giving this book to a terminally ill teenager, the adult must read the book first. Could be very helpful for a teenage boy.

The Courage to Grieve: Creative living, recovery and growth through grief

Judy Tatelbaum

Mandarin (1990) new edition   0 7493 0936 9   £5.99

This self-help book is divided into sections that include The Grief Experience, The Recovery Process, Grief Resolution and Self Help. The author is a Gestalt therapist and psychiatric social worker in the USA. There is information on how to understand the grief of children and how to help them. There is advice on how to help oneself and others. A large part of the book deals with how to get through the grief work, how to complete and finish the mourning, and be open to the change that recovery brings.

This could be a very helpful book for someone mourning, as well as for professionals wanting to help a child.

The Death of a Child – a book for families
Tessa Wilkinson
Julia MacRae Books, 1991　　　　　　1 85681 250 2　　　　　£7.99

Written by a bereavement counsellor at a children's hospice using her experience gained from working with parents and children and listening to their expressed needs and feelings. It is a short book of 79 pages, beautifully illustrated, written for bereaved families. The author writes with empathy and it is a very moving book, easy to read. There is an illustrated story to be read with a bereaved child about the death of a brother – what happens and some of the feelings. Finally, there are eleven pages of poems and prose extracts from authors such as C S Lewis, A A Milne, J R Tolkien as well as several from a Christian tradition.

Highly recommended for a family who has lost a child.

The Diddakoi
Rumer Godden
Pan, 1991　　　　　　　　　　0 330 32397 0　　　　　　£3.50

Seven year-old Kizzy is a diddakoi, a half-gypsy, who lived in a caravan with her Gran and their horse. She is tormented in school by the other girls because she is very different to them. When Gran suddenly dies the caravan is burnt, according to tradition. Kizzy has to learn to live in a house and adjust to a different way of life. She fights the adults and children around her at the same time as mourning her Gran and their life together. She gets badly bullied at school. Eventually her need of friendship and love help her overcome her difficulties.

A warm book about being an outsider and how people can come to care for each other. For older primary age children.

The Dying and Bereaved Teenager
Ed: John Morgan
The Charles Press, US, 1990　　　　　0 914783 44 0　　　　Out of print

The chapters are written for professionals by different experts. Part one is about the dying teenager and the role of professionals in an adolescent support group. Part two deals with the bereaved teenager and the impact of major life transitions on adolescent development. Part three is about the role of the school with guidelines for dealing with traumatic events, bereavement support groups for secondary students and suicide prevention in the school.

A book for those responsible for managing the pastoral care in a school.

The Dying Child: An annotated bibliography

Hazel B Benson

Greenwood Press, London, 1988   0 313 24708 0

This bibliography covers material written between 1960 and 1987 gathered from over 180 popular and professional journals in the fields of medicine, education, psychology and social work. Books, chapters in books, conference reports, government documents, pamphlets and doctoral dissertations are included. The entries are grouped according to major categories. The first section covers general aspects such as historical views, religious aspects, cultural beliefs, grief and mourning. The second section deals with the young child: concepts of death, communicating with the child, telling the child the diagnosis, psycho-social care of the dying child and the handicapped child. The third section deals with the adolescent, with case histories, psycho-social adaptations and communicating with the adolescent. The fourth section deals with the different categories of care givers. The final section deals with physical care: care in hospital, the symptoms and pain relief, parental participation in care, home care and hospice care. The appendices contain lists of books for children and audio-visual material. The references are mainly American.

This is a very extensive bibliography for a professional who wants to find references on a particular topic.

The Friends

Rosa Guy

Puffin Modern Classics, 1995   0 14 036616 4   £4.99

The book is set in Harlem, New York, and tells of a way of life that is unfamiliar to many readers in Britain. Phyllisia has been brought from the West Indies to Harlem by her father whom she hates. She feels an outsider and is badly bullied at school because of her accent and her ability to answer questions in class. The only person who wants to be her friend is the untidy, cheeky Edith whom Phyllisia despises. They eventually become friends and Phyllisia gets an insight into the harsh reality of her friend's life. After the death of Phyllisia's mother from cancer and with Edith having to face the death of three of her family members, Phyllisia slowly grows up and starts to understand the real value of those around her. She eventually even reaches out to the father that she has hated for so long.

This is not an easy book because of its portrayal of lifestyles where violence is commonplace. However, there is also affection. The pain of the bereavement and the effects on Phyllisia are described realistically.

May be especially helpful for a teenager from a similar ethnic background.

The Huge Bag of Worries
Virginia Ironside, Mark Mackenzie-Smith
The Royal Scottish Society for Prevention of Cruelty to Children,1994
Melville House, 1 Polwarth Terrace, Edinburgh EH11 1NU

This is a colourful booklet of 18 pages about Morna who has always been a happy girl but who has become more and more burdened by a huge bag of worries. It follows her everywhere and when she tries to ask people what to do, nobody listens. But Gran notices and together they sort out all the worries and they eventually vanish. The final advice is to share your worries with someone.

A very reassuring little book to encourage young children to share their worries. To read with a young child.

The Impact of AIDS: Understanding social issues series
Ewan Armstrong
Gloucester Press, 1990   0 7496 0119 1   £8.50

An information book with multi-cultural photographs for secondary school pupils written by a lecturer in Health Education who is personally involved with HIV.

The book starts with factual information about transmission and testing. The next chapter deals with some issues faced by people living with AIDS and HIV with quotes and a case study. Further chapters deal with global issues, community responses and looking towards the future. There is a list of sources of help as well as a glossary. The figures quoted are for 1989 and transmission through breast milk is not mentioned.

This book of about 60 easily read pages would be appropriate in secondary school libraries so that individual pupils can look up facts.

The Kingdom by the Sea

Robert Westall

Mammoth, 1992   0 7497 0796 8   £3.50

Thirteen year-old Harry survives a direct hit of a bomb on his house during the Second World War by getting to their garden dugout in time. His parents and little sister did not make it. After being rescued and seeing his home in ruins, he decides that he cannot bear to live with his aunt so, still in a state of shock, he runs away. He is befriended by a dog, bombed-out like himself. Together they move northwards along the coast of north-east England searching for shelter and ways of obtaining food. They learn not to trust everyone and to travel by night. But they also meet people who have become bereaved or are lonely, and through their kindness, they acquire survival skills.

At the end of the book, when Harry and his dog seem to have reached a haven, he discovers that his family did not die after all but were badly injured and then re-housed. Harry has to cope with the anger and disapproval expressed by his parents when he unexpectedly turns up. The ending is not rosy, but there is some hope that the kingdom by the sea that the two of them had discovered will still be there for him sometime in the future.

This is a well written and realistic book that deals with feelings. However, someone bereaved may find it difficult to accept that those who were assumed to be dead are, in fact, alive. For 9–14 year-olds.

The Last Battle

C S Lewis

Collins, 1990   0 00 674036 7   £3.99

This is the last book of the *Chronicles of Narnia* but it can be read without having read the previous books. There are references to previous adventures, but this story is complete in itself. It deals with the last battle between the good King Tirian and evil and cruel invaders of the peaceful Narnia. The king is helped by two human children from England who get summoned from one world to this one. The forces for good seem small and helpless as many of the inhabitants in Narnia are deceived and do not understand what is going on. In the last fierce battle, individuals get mortally wounded and they pass through a door in a hovel and instead of the darkness and fear they expected, they are in a sunny, calm and beautiful country. If you do what you feel is right when you have to make choices during your lifetime, you end up in this enchanted place where all those you have ever known and who have died are waiting to welcome you. It becomes clear that the two children from England had actually died in a train accident as well as in the Narnia battle. The last part of the book describes this new existence – where they had lived before was as if in a shadow land, now they are in the sunshine for ever and with those they love.

This might be an excellent book to read aloud with a bereaved child of upper primary school age.

The Tenth Good Thing About Barney
Judith Viorst
Collins, 1974   0 00 195 821 6   Out of print

"My cat Barney died last Friday. I was very sad. I cried and didn't watch television". The family has a funeral and bury Barney under a tree in the garden. The grief is helped by making a list of all the good things about Barney. There is conflict between the sisters as to where Barney is – in heaven or in the ground. Father plants some seeds that will change in the ground and grow with the help of Barney. This is the missing tenth good thing about Barney. A good book in that it encourages the making of a list of all the good things remembered.

A sensitive picture book with black and white drawings for 5-8 year-olds.

The Transformation of Jennifer
Howard Anthony Masters
Mammoth, 1993   0 7497 1478 6   £2.99

Jennifer's older brother Derek dies of AIDS in Kent after having contracted the infection through needle sharing while at university. Jennifer's world is destroyed as well as that of her parents. Being unable to accept help offered, she attempts suicide but is rescued by a boy of the same age who belongs to a small Christian community nearby. She escapes from the tension at home to this community where their calm acceptance of her starts to give her some peace of mind. There are some young people in the community struggling with their ambivalence about wanting to remain within it or to leave. Jennifer's father cannot accept that his daughter is seeking support and his anger is destructive. The book ends with an open question.

The book is written for older teenagers.

The Very Best of Friends
Margaret Wild, Julie Vivas
Bodley Head, 1990   0 370 31435 2   Out of print

William, the cat, lives with James, the young farmer, and Jessie, his wife. Jessie only just tolerates the cat but James loves him and they do the farm work together during the day and at night William is better than a hot water bottle on the bed. Then James suddenly dies. Jessie mourns and William, the cat, is excluded from the house even at night. Jessie gives up working on the farm and watches TV all day. William becomes a mean and lean cat hating everyone. One day he scratches Jessie when she feeds him scraps and Jessie suddenly notices how poorly William looks and invites him in. She suggests that they could get to know each other. They both start to work together and William ends up sleeping on her feet at night.

This is a large picture book with lovely illustrations dealing with the despair and depression after a bereavement but shows that you can adjust and together eventually return to activities of life. For 3–8 year-olds.

There Is Always Danny
Jean Ure
Corgi Freeway, 1989   0 552 52429 8   Out of print

The second book in a trilogy about four friends at a sixth form college specialising in drama. It is about living away from parents for the first time and falling in love. As a small side issue, an adult male friend of one of the class mates has had an AIDS diagnosis and Kate, the main person in the book, feels very mature as she is not rejecting his company. This sub-plot is very small. For teenagers.

There is a Rainbow behind every Dark Cloud

The Centre for Attitudinal Healing

1978, 19 Main Street, Tiburon, CA 94920, USA   0 89087 253 8

Eleven children share their experiences of terminal illness, especially the ways they help each other cope with the prospect of their own death. This is an A4 sized book of children's drawings and words with space for the child reading the book to draw their own feelings. The philosophy of the book is that healing or 'getting well' means being happy and peaceful inside, that healing takes place when we feel nothing but love inside and when we are no longer scared or feeling bad about anything. It means living each second as if it were the only time there is, making this day count.

The book could be used as a source of ideas for skilled facilitators to develop their own work with an individual child or a group of seriously ill children through the use of drawing and sharing thoughts.

Tiger Eyes

Judy Blume

Heinemann Educational, 1984   0 435 12278 9   £4.75

Life as she knew it was shattered for fifteen year-old Davey when her father was shot in his shop. In her grief and anger, she cuts herself off from her family and friends. She becomes frightened of the world. Davey, her mother and little brother are taken to New Mexico by an aunt and uncle. Her mother can no longer cope with her grief and their stay becomes longer as the family members slowly adjust to their loss. Through becoming the friend of a girl in her new school and an older boy whose father is dying of cancer, she finds ways of expressing her feelings. The family eventually decide to return home and continue with their lives.

This is a moving novel of how a teenage girl experiences grief and learns to cope. The author is a well known writer of teenage books. For mid-teens.

Two Weeks with the Queen

Morris Gleitzman

Pan Books, 1990   0 330 31376 2   £3.50

Colin, a young teenager has a younger brother, Luke, who is dying of leukaemia. His parents send Colin from Australia to relatives in London to avoid the distress. He tries to deal with his confused feelings by attempting to contact the Queen in order to find the best doctor there is to heal his brother. He is befriended by a gay couple where one partner is dying of AIDS, and through their friendship and shared feelings he comes to realise that his place is back home with his brother. He has grown up through this experience.

A moving story with funny incidents dealing with terminal illness and AIDS. The book has been read by thousands of young teenagers as part of their English curriculum in Lothian, read on TV and made into play. This is a well written book which is difficult to put down and is highly recommended. For young teenagers.

Under the Blackberries, In-between the Roses
Rachel Pank
All Books for Children, 1991   1 85406 127 5   £7.95

Sonia and Barnie the cat went everywhere and did everything together. One day Barnie wasn't there and Sonia looked everywhere. Dad told her that Barnie had died and Sonia couldn't do anything to bring him back. Sonia cried a lot and the family was kind to her. Nothing was the same without Barnie. The family buried Barnie in the garden and covered the grave with rose petals. Over the next few weeks, Sonia slowly cries less and less and can almost see Barnie at times in the garden. One day she gets a kitten and Sonia loves her but the rose bush over Barnie is a special place for Sonia and Barnie where the kitten can't play.

A lovely picture book full of details. For young primary age children.

Visit to a Hospital
Gillian Mercer, Peter Dennis
Kingfisher Read-About, 1992   0 86272 955 6   £3.99

Amy has a hernia and arrives at hospital to have an operation. The book contains information about all the different kinds of jobs that are done by people who work in hospitals, the different kinds of wards and treatment rooms. Different nurses perform medical procedures. There are drawings of a sphygmomanometer and a drip. The activities on the children's ward are detailed. Mum spends the night nearby. The activities during the night in the hospital are described. The staff in the operating theatre are introduced and what happens in the recovery room after the operation is described. Joe fell off a climbing frame and is brought to the Accident and Emergency Department and he has an X-ray. Both the children go home.

Several educational advisors and hospital staff have been involved in the development of this large hardback book. There is quite a lot of text on each double spread and very detailed, realistic drawings. This could be a very useful book for a slightly older child who is going into hospital.

Water Bugs and Dragonflies – Explaining death to children
Doris Stickney, Gloria Oritz

Mowbray (1994) new edition   0 264 66904 5   £0.99

The water bugs wonder what happens to each of their friends who have climbed up the stem of a pond lily and never returned. One spring day one of them climbed up and emerged as a dragonfly. The attempt to return to tell the others failed as he could no longer re-enter the water. He would have to wait until the others joined him. So 'he winged off happily into the wonderful new world of sun and air'.

The straightforward illustrated story is followed by a prayer for the child to say. There are then some pages in smaller print for parents on what to say to children. This is followed by three quotes from the Bible and a prayer for parents.

This is a small booklet with detailed monochrome illustrations on each double page. Even a non-Christian family can use the story with a dying child or a sibling. Could be read with a very young child as well as older primary school age children.

We Love Them
Martin Waddell, Barbara Firth

Walker Books, 1991   0 7445 1774 5   £3.50

Ben, the dog, finds a lost rabbit in the snow and the children bring it home. Ben thinks it is a young dog and the rabbit thinks Ben is a big rabbit. Ben cares for the rabbit together with the children. The rabbit grows. One day Ben dies of old age. Grief is felt by all the family and the rabbit refuses to eat. A new puppy is brought and cared for by the rabbit and the children.

Simple, repetitive language and soft and lovely pictures illustrate the rural setting of this story – a story that could be read over and over again. To be read with very young children and for slightly older ones.

We're Talking about AIDS

Karen Bryant Mole

Wayland, 1994   0 7502 1705 7   £4.50

This book is for middle and upper primary school age children with photographs and diagrams. There are useful chapters on what a virus is, how the immune system works, and how HIV is transmitted. It does however wrongly state that the blood of mother and baby is shared but does not explain why most babies, born of infected mothers are not themselves infected. The book mentions transmission through sex and has diagrams of male and female sex organs and talks about condoms for protection. There is a chapter that asks why people who are infected did not protect themselves. The people who are photographed state that they did not think it could happen to them. The book deals with what happens when you are infected, whether it shows, what it feels like, counselling and research. There is a glossary.

Parents in families with HIV have found this a useful book to read with their children. It is also a very useful book for any primary school library.

What Can I Do About AIDS

Barnardo's/The Terrence Higgins Trust

Barnardo's, 1993

Tanners Lane, Barkingside, Ilford, Essex IG6 1QG,

The Terrence Higgins Trust, 52–54 Grays Inn Road, London WC1X 8JU

A booklet of ten pages written for younger teenagers who want to learn about AIDS. It is also written for children in a family where someone is infected with HIV and mentions how they can try to find support. A useful elementary pamphlet for older children that concentrates on how you do not become infected and the need to understand and support someone you know who is infected. It is easy to read with colourful cartoons and a photo story. For younger teenagers.

What's a Virus Anyway – The kids' book about AIDS

David Fassler, Kelly McQueen

Waterfront Books (1990) 1994   0 914525 15 8   Out of print

This American book is designed to help parents and teachers talk about AIDS with young children between 5 and 12 years of age. It provides basic information about AIDS. The author leaves out details on sexual transmission as he feels that information about sex to a young child should not be associated with a disease.

The large pages have a question written by a child on one page and an answer for the adult to talk through on the opposite page. It is an interactive book where the child is encouraged to draw on the pages. The child is asked to draw a virus and a white blood cell without any previous information. On the pages following a request for a drawing there are pen drawings done by children. The book introduces illnesses caused by different viruses. The three transmission routes of HIV are stated as well as a list of ways in which you cannot become infected.

The book states that people with AIDS are like everybody else. Some people can live for years or even longer whilst others get very sick and die in a short time. The child is told to talk with their parents, teachers, doctor or school nurse if they feel scared or worried about AIDS.

The resource list refers to American and Canadian groups only. For primary age children.

When Dad Died

Sheila Hollins, Lester Sireling

St George's Mental Health Library, 1994   1 874439 06 0   £9.50

The simple pictures tell about the death of Dad in a straightforward account of Dad feeling pain, the ambulance coming, visiting Dad in hospital, Dad being dead, the funeral and the family living on. The story is centred round Stephen who could be in his late teens. There are illustrations about how he is feeling sad and cries, feeling cross and muddled and angry. The sentences are short and the book can be used for primary aged children as well as with young adults with special educational needs. There is a similar book, *When Mum Died*.

When Dad Died – Working through loss with people who have learning disabilities or with children

Sheila Hollins, Lester Sireling

St George's Mental Health Library, 1994   4830 01 6/343   Complete set £125.00

An aid to one-to-one bereavement counselling for parents to help prepare children for an anticipated death and to help children work through the memories of a loss at a later date. It can also be used for staff training sessions. There are stimulus pictures, work cards, training material in a ring binder as well as five copies of *When Dad Died*, and a full colour booklet reproducing the pictures plus accompanying text.

When Mum Died

Sheila Hollins, Lester Sireling

St George's Mental Health Library, 1994   1 874439 07 0   £9.50

Similar to *When Dad Died*. It is a straightforward account of Mum having a pain, going to hospital, dying, seeing her in the coffin, the funeral and the family continuing as a family. The illustrations are clear and colourful and there is a simple text of only one or two sentences on each double page. Stephen, the son, is drawn as a young teenager and his feelings and experiences are clear in words and pictures. This book can be used both for young children and especially with young adults with special educational needs.

When my Brother Died – a little book to help parents and children come to terms with bereavement

Anthea Dove, Antoinette Hastings

Catholic Truth Society, 1987   0 85183 664 X   £0.75

'I know Tom is with God, so he must be happy'. Tom was 12 and his brother 11 when Tom died two years earlier. At the funeral, his brother felt like a lump of stone. He only cried when Tom's football rolled out from under the bed. He was comforted by Mum and Dad who were both crying. The family felt close. The brother gets angry with God but Father Pat comes to see the family and says that God had given them the happiness of being with the wonderful boy Tom had been for twelve years. Now he is with God and he is loved and happy.

This is a small booklet of 15 pages with a simple illustration on each double page for young primary age children. It could be helpful in a Christian family.

When Parents Die – A book for teenagers and young adults
Rebecca Abrams
Thorsons, 1995   0 7225 3131 1   £9.95

The book is written for older teenagers and young adults whose parents died while they were still growing up. The author lost both her father and step-father within two years, in her late teens, and found that her feelings and expressions of grief were misunderstood or ignored by others. She did not consider asking for help as she assumed no-one would understand. Other young adults have contributed their experiences when they lost a parent. There are chapters on the period around the bereavement, the time-span of grief, changes and losses that may trigger renewed distress, and the expression of grief in other forms such as abusing alcohol, taking drugs or developing eating problems. The author writes about letting go and getting on without abandoning the memories of the parent who has died. There is a reading list.

This could be a very supportive book for older teenagers.

When People Die
Guinevere Williams, Julia Ross
Macdonald Publishers, 1983   0 904265 76 5   Out of print

This is written in a language easy to read for upper primary school children and maybe early secondary school pupils with 48 pages on 'Why people die', 'What is death', 'What has to be done', 'Facing loss' and 'Coping with loss and helping others'. There are notes on funerals, beliefs and rituals both for Christians and people of other faiths. The last chapter raises the issues of death from abortion, euthanasia and suicide through simple case stories that are left open ended for discussion. There is also a glossary of terms.

This is an informative book that aims to set out the facts clearly and sympathetically and should be in primary and secondary school libraries. It would not be appropriate to use it to help a bereaved child: this book should be read beforehand.

When Someone has a very Serious Illness – Children can learn how to cope with loss and change

Marge Heegaard

Woodland Press US, 1991
99 Woodland Circle,
Minneapolis, MN 55424, USA   0 9620502 4 5   £6.50

A very helpful workbook to be filled in and illustrated by 5–12 year-olds together with an adult. The *Facilitator Guide for Drawing out Feelings* by the same author provides a short theoretical background to working with children as well as what equipment is needed for each session and a clear plan of how to organise it.

When Someone very Special Dies – Children can learn to cope with grief

Marge Heegaard

Woodland Press US, 1991
99 Woodland Circle,
Minneapolis, MN 55424, USA   0 9620502 0 2   £6.50

A very helpful workbook to be filled in and illustrated by 5–12 year-olds together with an adult. The *Facilitator Guide for Drawing out Feelings* by the same author provides a short theoretical background to working with children as well as what equipment is needed for each session and a clear plan of how to organise it.

When Someone you Love has AIDS – A book of hope for family and friends

Betty Clare Moffatt

IBS Press, US, 1986   0 9616605 03   Out of print

The book is a personal account of the agony felt by a mother whose adult son has AIDS in America in the early 1980s. The author worked as a counsellor and the book contains heart rending accounts of other men with AIDS. It was written when the AIDS epidemic was new and reflects some of the issues then.

When Something Terrible Happens – Children can learn to cope with grief

Marge Heegaard

Woodland Press, Minneapolis, 1991
99 Woodland Circle,
Minneapolis, MN 55424, USA   0 9620502 3 7   £6.50

A very helpful workbook to be filled in and illustrated by 5–12 year-olds together with an adult. The *Facilitator Guide for Drawing out Feelings* by the same author provides a short theoretical background to working with children as well as what equipment is needed for each session and a clear plan of how to organise it.

When Uncle Bob Died

Althea

Dinosaur Publications, 1988   0 85122 727 9   £1.75

'I found a butterfly on the windowsill. Mum said it was dead'. Mum tells the little boy that when you play war, death is only pretence. But the butterfly will not fly again. All animals and people will have to die one day. When Uncle Bob died after an illness, he was not old. People felt angry and sad. There was a funeral. Uncle Bob's children came to play. The family talked about Uncle Bob and their good memories. When Dad was ill, the little boy got frightened that Dad would also die but he got better. Mum reminded the boy that people live on through the memories.

An excellent book, nicely illustrated for younger primary age children.

Wise Before the Event – Coping with crisis in schools

William Yule, Anne Gold

Calouste Gulbenkian Foundation, 1993
Turnabout Distribution Ltd,
27 Horsell Road, London N5 1XL   0 903319 66 7   £5.00

The ways in which unexpected disasters and crises such as major loss following a fire, injuries and deaths of pupils can affect school are described with suggestions about how schools can help to lessen the physical and emotional effects of such disasters. Many of the strategies suggested can be built into the curriculum of every school. Case examples are given from the

Herald of Free Enterprise, Jupiter and the Hillsborough disasters as well as the deaths of a teacher and a pupil in accidents.

A very useful little book of 62 pages for teachers, easy to read and well worth trying to locate. It has been mailed to all schools in the UK.

Wise Before their Time – Stories of people living with AIDS and HIV

Ed: Ann Richardson, Dietmar Bolle

Fount Publications, 1992   0 00 627648 2   £4.99

The book consists of a series of personal statements made by individuals from different countries living with HIV under a number of headings eg: Getting tested, Telling others, and Early thoughts. All the contributions are from adults and the book is for adults.

You and HIV, One Day at a Time – For children with HIV (and other people)

Lynn Baker

W B Saunders, US, 1991   0 7216 3606 3   £16.00

This is a book for children with HIV, their parents but also for teachers, social workers, policy makers and those interested in children with HIV infection. It contains facts, feelings and issues, clinical manifestations of HIV infection and its treatment in detail. The book is written to give children living with HIV a chance to know what is going on and thus to participate and live positively, and by helping the people who care about them learn enough to be able to answer the questions they may ask.

Each page has only a few sentences and line drawings. It starts with simple diagrams of cells, genes and different organ systems and moves on to talk about blood and then the immune system and the functions of different white cells. The different tests that are done are explained such as HIV antibody test, antigen test, HIV cultures, PCR test and the purpose of different blood counts. The author then goes on to describe stages of HIV infection, symptoms and different treatments. There is space for the child to fill in their own treatment plan.

It acknowledges the worry, sadness and troubled feelings in the family, and the wish to live a long time. It deals with the need to share feelings with others. There is an extensive reference section dealing with medical procedures, what happens and why they are done. There is a Glossary and an Index to make it easier to look up and read about a particular fact, treatment or drug.

The child is encouraged to live a day at a time, hopefully feeling good most of the time. This is not a book to read in one sitting but a reference book for all the members of the family over the years. It is the most informative factual book for non specialists available at the moment. It is written using an easy language and cheerful diagrams but all the technical terms are there and they are explained. It is a very useful book written with compassion and knowledge by a psychiatrist.

The author thinks that children even younger than 10 years of age could read and understand parts of the text but even adults would find the content exhaustive.

Young People and Bereavement

The Hospice of St Francis

The Hospice of St Francis, 1990
27 Shrublands Road, Berkhamstead, Herts HP4 3HX

Five pages with mono-colour line drawings. There are short statements such as: "I can't believe it's happened", "I feel so guilty", and "No-one can help me" each followed by a response of three or four sentences. The Helplines on the last page are all in England.

This could be a very useful little leaflet to hand to a teenager at the early stages of bereavement.

Your Friend, Rebecca

Linda Hoy

Beaver Books (1983) new editon   0 09 931280 8   £2.99

Rebecca's mother died a year ago. Rebecca isn't anybody's friend, everybody picks on her at her secondary school. At home, her Dad hardly notices that she exists and the two of them act as if they were strangers. Rebecca is angry and rebellious at school but through Drama classes she slowly starts to get in contact with some of her feelings. She slowly discovers that her Dad is reacting with grief to the loss of his wife yet neither of them has been able to notice the distress of the other. Once she has allowed herself to listen to the support that is available and starts to release some of the pent-up feelings, the relationships both with her father and others at school start to repair. The book ends with Rebecca and her Dad facing the future together, both much more aware of how to support each other. A powerful book that could be given to a teenager suffering bereavement who may be able to recognise Rebecca's feelings and situations as their own.

Highly recommended for young teenagers.

Your Parent has Died

Bryony Jacklin

Department of Social Work, St Christopher's Hospice, 1991
51–59 Lawrie Park Road, London SE26 6DZ

A small monochrome booklet of eight pages that deals, in a couple of paragraphs under each illustration, with questions or statements such as: Why did this happen to me?, Why now?, Everything's changed, Is it OK to forget about it sometimes?, Things I didn't say, and Do and Don't.

A helpful and gentle book for middle primary school children and young teenagers.

Author list

The **Paediatric AIDS Resource Centre** aims to improve the care of children and families affected by HIV/AIDS by: responding to telephone, written and personal enquiries; organising training courses designed to promote good practice; holding annual Scientific Updates on HIV in Women and Children for practitioners; publishing and distributing leaflets and books.

The following **Parent Information Leaflets** written by Jacqueline Mok, Consultant Paediatrician and Fiona Mitchell, Specialist Health Visitor, are available from PARC:

- I am HIV positive. What does this mean for my child?
- My child is infected. How do you know?
- My child is infected. Where do you go from here?
- My child is infected. Signs and symptoms.
- My child is infected. What treatments are available?
- Infants and Children at risk of HIV – Guidance notes for carers.

Maybe Another Day 1 900339 00 5
The first of four interactive booklets for 3–7 year-olds, colourfully illustrated, with a simple storyline encouraging children affected by parental illness to talk through worrying or troublesome issues with a trusted adult.

PARC is soon to publish a resource pack of interactive materials for working with affected 8–12 year-olds with sections on:

- Me and my family
- Family business (secrets and confidential matters)
- The Virus
- Changes (preparation for separation, foster care)
- Feelings (to allow children to express emotions)
- Illness in the family
- Loss and bereavement

Further information from:
PARC Edinburgh,
Department of Child Life and Health
20 Sylvan Place
Edinburgh EH9 1UW
Tel: 0131 536 0806
Fax: 0131 536 0841